W9-BKS-783

Complete Book
of Wedding
Vows

Also by Diane Warner

How to Have a Big Wedding on a Small Budget

*Big Wedding on a Small Budget
Planner and Organizer*

*Beautiful Wedding Decorations and Gifts
on a Small Budget*

*How to Have a Fabulous, Romantic
Honeymoon on a Budget*

The Best Wedding Ever

Complete Book
of Wedding
Vows

By
Diane Warner

AUG 0 7 2003 PORTER COUNTY PUBLIC LIBRARY SYSTEM

NEW PAGE BOOKS
A division of The Career Press, Inc.
Franklin Lakes, NJ

Hebron Public Library

habnf   HEB
392.5 WARNE

Warner, Diane
Complete book of wedding vows
33410007161757   09/25/17

Copyright © 1996 by Diane Warner

All rights reserved under the Pan-American and International Copyright Conventions. This book may not be reproduced, in whole or in part, in any form or by any means electronic or mechanical, including photocopying, recording, or by any information storage and retrieval system now known or hereafter invented, without written permission from the publisher, The Career Press.

COMPLETE BOOK OF WEDDING VOWS
Cover photo by Michael Krasowitz/FPG International
Cover design by Dean Johnson Design, Inc.
Printed in the U.S.A. by Book-mart Press

To order this title, please call toll-free 1-800-CAREER-1 (NJ and Canada: 201-848-0310) to order using VISA or Master Card, or for further information on books from Career Press.

The Career Press, Inc., 3 Tice Road, PO Box 687, Franklin Lakes, NJ 07417
www.careerpress.com
www.newpagebooks.com

Library of Congress Cataloging-in-Publication Data

Warner, Diane.
  Complete book of wedding vows / by Diane Warner.
     p.   cm.
  Includes index.
  ISBN 1-56414-237-X (pbk.)
  1. Marriage service.   I. Title.
BL619.M37W37   1996
392'.5--dc21   96-13890
                                                      CIP

Dedication

With love to my granddaughter, Renee.

Acknowledgments

My thanks go to all of those who shared their vows with me for this book, including hundreds of newlyweds and dozens of ministers, priests and rabbis. I would especially like to thank the Reverend Father John Magoulias of the Greek Orthodox Church, Dr. John E. Stensether of the Evangelical Free Church of America and Rabbi Stuart Dauermann of the Ahavat Zion Messianic Synagogue. I would also like to thank my daughter, Lynn Paden, as well as my friend, Helen Christy, who took their valuable time to help me with the monumental task of collecting newlyweds' wedding vows. Extra special thanks go to those couples who not only shared their vows but their love stories, as well: Andrew and Karen Goldberg; Ben and Wendi King; Joel and Colleen Blomenkamp; Joseph and Kathleen McLaughlin; Eric Wood and Kim Gray; Warren and Verna Riopel; Bill and Kathy Moran; Loren and Erma Hosmer; and my son and daughter-in-law, Darren and Lisa Warner.

Contents

Introduction

The essence of every wedding is the recitation of the vows. Without the vows themselves, the wedding day would be nothing more than a big party, a celebration of the couple's love for each other. The bride may be radiant as she glides down the aisle in her expensive designer gown, the massive cathedral may be opulently decorated from floor to rafters and the professional musicians may bring tears to the eyes of your guests. But without the wedding vows, it is all a silly waste of time and money.

Wedding vows have not always been part of the marriage ceremony, however. As we look back into history we find all manner of humorous, peculiar and totally bizarre ways to marry. As far back as the earliest accounts of ancient Greeks, Romans, Jews, Medes and Persians, marriages were arranged as a matter of practicality and common sense. The modern concept of romantic love had no part in these marriages, which were arranged for legal, financial and social reasons, and only rarely did the ceremonies have any religious significance. No wonder brides wore heavy veils to hide their faces until after the ceremony!

Those of you who love historical romance novels have probably chuckled at the barbaric methods of marriage by capture, and it may seem as if this was something from the long distant past. However, marriage by capture was still legal in England until the 13th century, as well as in other countries around the world. In some of the old provinces of India, in fact, a Kanjar groom would gather his friends and arm them with muskets, stones and sticks, then descend on the home of his chosen bride. The fight would continue until the bride's family finally gave her over to the Kanjar groom.

And then there are the stories of the Australasian tribesmen who "married" the maidens of their choice by simply shooting barbless arrows through their legs—talk about a wedding on a small budget! Even the early Christians did not give marriage any religious significance until about the year 537 (common era), and the Catholics held out even longer; they decided to make marriage a religious ceremony after the Council of Trent in 1563.

The American wedding of today, however, evolved from two great civilizations, Rome and Greece, where the bride wore a veil and was given a wedding ring by her groom; the couple ate a special cake and rice was thrown as the groom carried the bride over the threshold of his home. Also, ceremony vows, as we know them today, emanated from the early Roman wedding. The Roman bride stood in her wedding costume, which consisted of a hemless tunic tied by a woolen girdle around her waist, fastened with a special knot called the Knot of Hercules. Over this tunic she wore a yellow cloak that matched her yellow sandals, and around her neck she wore a metal necklace. Over all of this she added a veil of red or yellow and on the crown of her head she wore a wreath of myrtle and orange blossoms. Finally, when she was thoroughly dressed, she stood with her family and welcomed her groom. At this point an animal was sacrificed, usually a sheep or a pig, after which the couple joined hands and stood before a pronuba, a Roman priestess, where they publicly pledged themselves to each other, probably the first official recitation of the wedding vow.

Wedding vows were also mentioned in the Bible; Hebrews 13:4 exhorts us to honor our marriage and its vows. But today, the wedding vow has become the *heart* of the marriage ceremony. In fact, it is said to be the highest vow known to mankind.

Throughout American history the wording of wedding vows was quite traditional, carefully treasured and preserved by ministers, priests and rabbis. Whenever these clergymen were called on to perform a wedding, the bride and groom accepted the traditional wording without question. Finally, in the 1950s and 1960s, and especially during the era of the barefooted flower children who took the formal marriage ceremony out of the sanctuary and onto the hillsides, wedding vows began to evolve from the traditional to the nontraditional. In fact, today most couples personalize their vows, composing them from their hearts to express their deep feelings of love and commitment to each other.

This book offers the formal, traditional wedding vows, along with hundreds of personalized nontraditional vows, including those used in second marriages, marriages of older couples, ceremonies of reaffirmation and weddings involving children from previous marriages.

There are also chapters that offer vows with religious variations, vows inspired by the classics and one devoted solely to ring vows. And just for fun, I've also sprinkled a few "up close and personal" love stories throughout the book that not only include the couples' personalized vows, but how they met and fell in love.

You'll find that today's vows are written in three different ways: question-answer format; monologue format; or the very popular dialogue format, in which the bride and groom alternate phrases. As you consider the vows offered in this book, you may select one of them as your own, or you may, as the majority of couples prefer to do, use them to whet your creative juices as you write your own unique vows to each other.

Because this book contains the largest compilation of vows ever assembled, it should be read slowly and savored thoughtfully, and it may help if you highlight the words, phrases or complete vow segments you especially like as you read along. This will make it easier for you to choose your favorite vow or to create your own. You'll see what I mean as you're reading along and certain phrases just seem to click as you say to yourself, "Yes! That's exactly the way I feel deep down in my heart."

I want your wedding to be special! God bless you as you plan it and especially as you write your vows, the most important and precious part of your ceremony.

Chapter 1

Traditional Vows

Throughout history, traditional wedding vows have been structured out of time-honored societal and religious values. In fact, in the past, and up until the 1950s, brides and grooms were willing to accept these traditional vows without question. In a sense, they willingly surrendered their union to the care and approbation of the larger community. This chapter gives many of these traditional vow phrasings from various faiths and nationalities.

Jewish

No single set of rules applies to all Jewish weddings because of the differences between the Orthodox, Conservative and Reform branches of the faith. In fact, individual rabbis and synagogues make their own interpretations. In the Orthodox and Conservative wedding services, an ancient Aramaic vow is usually recited before the groom places the ring on his bride's finger. This ring vow also serves as the groom's wedding vow. In the Sephardic transliteration, it reads:

> *"Harey at mekuddeshet li B'taba'at zo k'dat Moshe V'israel"*

which means:

> *"Behold thou are consecrated unto me with this ring according to the law of Moses and of Israel."*

In a double-ring ceremony, the bride presents a ring to her groom in the same way, reciting a slightly different vow.

Or for a Conservative service, these vows are often used, as taken from the *Rabbinical Assembly Manual* and published by the Rabbinical Assembly of America:

> *Rabbi (addressing the bridegroom): "Do you, _____, take _____ to be your lawful wedded wife, to love, to honor and to cherish?"*

> *Bridegroom: "I do."*

> *Rabbi (addressing the bride): "Do you, _____, take _____ to be your lawful wedded husband to love, to honor and to cherish?"*

> *Bride: "I do."*

Rabbi (addressing the bridegroom): "Then, do you,
_____, *put this ring upon the finger of*
your bride and say to her: 'Be thou consecrated to
me, as my wife, by this ring, according to the Law of
Moses and of Israel.' "

The Rabbi then asks the bride to repeat the following:

"May this ring I receive from thee be a token of my
having become thy wife according to the Law of
Moses and of Israel."

If two rings are used, the bride may say:

"This ring is a symbol that thou art my husband in
accordance with the Law of Moses and Israel."

In a Reformed service there is a distinctly separate wedding vow that is read by the rabbi and affirmed by the
bride and groom:

"O God, supremely blessed, supreme in might and
glory, guide and bless this groom and bride.
Standing here in the presence of God, the Guardian
of the home, ready to enter into the bond of wedlock,
answer in the fear of God, and in the hearing of
those assembled:

*Do you, _ _____, of your own free will and
consent take _____ to be your wife / husband
and do you promise to love, honor, and cherish
her / him throughout life?"*

Groom / bride: "I do."

The Seven Blessings are also a traditional part of any Jewish
marriage ceremony:

*"You Abound in Blessings, Adonai our God, who
created the fruit of the vine.*

*"You Abound in Blessings, Adonai our God. You
created all things for Your glory.*

*"You Abound in Blessings, Adonai our God. You
created humanity.*

*"You Abound in Blessings, Adonai our God. You
made humankind in Your image, after Your
likeness, and You prepared from us a perpetual
relationship. You abound in Blessings, Adonai our
God. You created humanity.*

*"May she who was barren rejoice when her children
are united in her midst in joy. You Abound in
Blessings, Adonai our God, who makes Zion rejoice
with her children.*

*"You make these beloved companions greatly rejoice
even as You rejoiced in Your creation in the Garden
of Eden as of old. You Abound in Blessings, Adonai
our God, who makes the bridegroom and bride to
rejoice.*

"You Abound in Blessings, Adonai our God, who created joy and gladness, bridegroom and bride, mirth and exultation, pleasure and delight, love, fellowship, peace, and friendship. Soon may there be heard in the cities of Judah and in the streets of Jerusalem, the voice of joy and gladness, the voice of the bridegroom and the voice of the bride, the jubilant voice of bridegrooms from their canopies and of youths from their feasts of song. You Abound in Blessings, Adonai our God. You make the bridegroom rejoice with the bride."

Catholic

The Catholic Church in America, also called the Roman Catholic Church, or the Church of Rome, follows strict doctrinal traditions, including those pertaining to the marriage ceremony. Although adherence to these traditions may vary slightly according to each individual parish priest's interpretation, there is usually very little deviation from tradition. This is especially true when the vows are recited during a wedding mass. Here are two examples of generally acceptable vow phrasings:

"I, _____, take you, _____, for my lawful wife / husband, to have and to hold, from this day forward, for better, for worse, for richer, for poorer, in sickness and health, until death do us part."

or:

"I,_____, take you, _____, to be my husband/wife. I promise to be true to you in good times and in bad, in sickness and in health. I will love and honor you all the days of my life."

Eastern Orthodox

The churches of the Eastern Rite (including Greek and Russian Orthodox) are similar in some ways to the Catholic Church. The marriage itself is a long ceremony rich with symbolism. An Orthodox wedding begins with a betrothal ritual that includes the Blessing and Exchange of Rings. The rings are exchanged between bride and groom three times to signify the Holy Trinity. At the close of this betrothal ritual, there is the Marriage Rite, including the Candles and the Joining of Hands, followed by the Crowning, the Cup and, finally, the Triumphal Procession of Isaiah. The vows themselves are spoken silently during this service, but the couple is considered married when the crowns are finally removed by the priest and he blesses them by saying:

"Be thou magnified, O bridegroom."

Muslim

It is forbidden for a Muslim woman to marry a non-Muslim. A Muslim man, however, may marry a non-Muslim woman. A traditional Muslim wedding requires a formal betrothal to take place, followed by a marriage contract and then the wedding ceremony itself, where these vows are spoken:

> *Bride: "I, _____, offer you myself in marriage in accordance with the instructions of the Holy Qur'an and the Holy Prophet, peace and blessing be upon Him. I pledge, in honesty and with sincerity, to be for you an obedient and faithful wife."*

> *Groom: "I pledge, in honesty and sincerity, to be for you a faithful and helpful husband."*

Hinduism

Hinduism is a religion native to India, broadly characterized by—among others—beliefs in reincarnation, a supreme being with many forms and natures, and a desire for liberation from earthly evils. Here is a modern-day interpretation of the traditionally strict Indian wedding vows:

> *"Let us take the first steps to provide for our household a nourishing and pure diet, avoiding those foods injurious to healthy living. Let us take the second step to develop physical, mental, and spiritual powers. Let us take the third step, to increase our wealth by righteous means and proper use. Let us take the fourth step, to acquire knowledge, happiness and harmony by mutual*

*love and trust. Let us take the fifth step, so that
we be blessed with strong, virtuous, and heroic
children. Let us take the sixth step, for self-
restraint and longevity. Finally, let us take the
seventh step and be true companions and remain
lifelong partners by this wedlock."*

An Indian wedding ritual is extremely complex and often
performed under a *bedi*, or outdoor shrine. A priest, on be-
half of the bride and groom, makes prayers and offerings,
followed by ceremonial rituals, including four circlings
around a sacred fire and the nuptial pole. Near the end of
the ceremony the priest ties the groom's sash to the bride's
veil and the couple exchanges their wedding vows, which
include these traditional Hindu phrasings from the ritual
of Seven Steps:

*"We have taken the Seven Steps. You have become
mine forever. Yes, we have become partners. I
have become yours. Hereafter, I cannot live
without you. Do not live without me. Let us share
the joys. We are word and meaning, united. You
are thought and I am sound. May the nights be
honey-sweet for us; may the mornings be honey-
sweet for us; may the earth be honey-sweet for us;
may the heavens be honey-sweet for us. May the
plants be honey-sweet for us; may the sun be all
honey for us; may the cows yield us honey-sweet
milk! As the heavens are stable, as the earth is
stable, as the mountains are stable, as the whole
universe is stable, so may our union be
permanently settled."*

♥ ♥ ♥ ♥

Carpatho-Russian Orthodox

This is a sect within the Eastern Orthodox Church that allows spoken vows, as opposed to the traditional silent vows taken during most Eastern Orthodox wedding ceremonies. Carpatho-Russian Orthodox marriage ceremonies are always quite formal, however.

> *"I, _____, take you, _____, as my wedded wife / husband and I promise you love, honor and respect; to be faithful to you, and not to forsake you until death do us part. So help me God, one in the Holy Trinity, and all the Saints."*

♥ ♥ ♥ ♥

Buddhism

Buddhism is the predominant religion of eastern and central Asia, represented by many differing sects that profess faith in the complex doctrines of Gautoma Buddha. This is a traditional Buddhist marriage homily:

> *"In the future, happy occasions will come as surely as the morning. Difficult times will come as surely as night. When things go joyously, meditate according to the Buddhist tradition. When things go badly, meditate. Meditation in the manner of the Compassionate Buddha will guide your life. To say the words 'love and compassion' is easy. But to accept that love and*

*compassion are built upon patience and
perseverance is not easy..."*

Episcopalian

The Episcopalian Church in the United States is also
known as the Protestant Episcopal Church, a body origi-
nally associated with the Church of England. This denomination tends to favor formal, traditional worship services
and wedding ceremonies.

*"In the Name of God, I _____, take you,
_____, to be my husband / wife, to have and
to hold from this day forward, for better, for worse,
for richer, for poorer, in sickness and in health, to
love and to cherish, until we are parted by death.
This is my solemn vow."*

or:

*"I, _____, take thee, _____, to
be my wedded husband / wife, to have and to hold
from this day forward, for better, for worse, for
richer, for poorer, in sickness and in health, to
love and to cherish, till death do us part,
according to God's holy ordinance; and thereto I
plight / give thee my troth."*

♥ ♥ ♥ ♥

American Lutheran

The American Lutheran Church branched out from the original Lutheran Church, a Protestant denomination founded by Martin Luther after the Reformation in the 16th century. There are many types of Lutheran churches in America, some favoring formal, traditional worship services, others a more relaxed, contemporary style, but all adhering to the Protestant religious teachings of Martin Luther. A Lutheran wedding ceremony may be formal or informal. This is one traditionally accepted wedding vow:

> *"I take you, _____, to be my*
> *husband / wife from this day forward, to join with*
> *you and share all that is to come, and I promise*
> *to be faithful to you until death parts us."*

Presbyterian

Although there are many types of Presbyterian churches, they all generally adhere to Calvinism, which is based on the religious doctrines of John Calvin, a 16th-century French theologian and religious reformer. As is true in the Lutheran church, Presbyterian churches vary greatly in their style of worship. In the case of a formal Presbyterian wedding ceremony, however, this is an example of an acceptable vow phrasing:

> *"I, _____, take you to be my wedded*
> *wife / husband, and I do promise and covenant,*
> *before God and these witnesses, to be your loving*

and faithful wife/husband, in plenty and in want, in joy and in sorrow, in sickness and in health, as long as we both shall live."

Methodist

The Methodist Church in America is a Protestant Christian denomination with theologies developed from the teachings of John and Charles Wesley. Their worship services, as well as their marriage ceremonies, vary greatly as to their formality. Here is one of their traditionally accepted wedding vows:

"In the Name of God, I, _____, take you, _____, to be my husband/wife, to have and to hold from this day forward, for better, for worse, for richer, for poorer, in sickness and in health, to love and to cherish, until we are parted by death. This is my solemn vow."

United Church of Christ

Although the United Church of Christ is a fairly new denomination in America, founded in 1957 by a merger of the Congregational Christian Church and the Evangelical and Reformed Church, they are direct descendants of the first permanent Protestant settlers—the Pilgrims. In their present *Book of Worship*, published in 1986, their denomination's preferred wedding vows are stated, reflecting the important concept of *giving* one's self, as different from *taking* another. Their vows are:

(Bride)

"_____ *(Groom's name), I give myself to you to be
your wife. I promise to love and sustain you in the
covenant of marriage, from this day forward, in
sickness and in health, in plenty and in want, in joy
and in sorrow, as long as we both shall live.*"

(Groom)

"_____ *(Bride's name), I give myself to you to be
your husband. I promise to love and sustain you in
the covenant of marriage, from this day forward, in
sickness and in health, in plenty and in want, in joy
and in sorrow, as long as we both shall live.*"

♥ ♥ ♥ ♥

Unitarian

The Unitarian Church does not offer a standard service, but
leaves the composition of the service to each of its ministers. Here are two examples, however, of typical Unitarian-
Universalist wedding vows:

The minister asks the bride and groom:

"_____, *will you take* _____
*to be your husband/wife; love, honor and cherish
him/her now and forevermore?*"

The bride and groom answer:

"I will."

Then the minister asks the bride and groom to repeat
these words:

*"I,_____, take you, _____,
to be my husband / wife; to have and to hold from
this day forward, for better, for worse, for richer,
for poorer, in sickness and in health, to love and
cherish always."*

The minister asks the bride and groom:

*"_____, will you have _____ to
be your husband / wife, to live together in creating
an abiding marriage? Will you love and honor,
comfort and cherish him / her in sickness and in
health, in sorrow and in joy, from this day
forward?"*

The bride and groom answer:

"I will."

♥ ♥ ♥ ♥

Quaker

A Quaker wedding is very simple, in keeping with the
Quaker tradition. The marriage usually takes places during a regular worship meeting where all in attendance
meditate silently while the bride and groom enter and join
those already seated. Then, after the traditional Quaker
silence, the bride and groom rise, join hands, face each
other and repeat these vows:

*"In the presence of God and these our Friends I
take thee to be my wife / husband, promising with*

Divine assistance to be unto thee a loving and faithful wife / husband so long as we both shall live."

The groom speaks his promises first, then the bride. The bride is not given away, nor does a third person pronounce them married, for the Friends believe that only God can create such a union.

Traditional nondenominational Protestant

There are hundreds of Protestant churches in America that are not affiliated with any particular denomination. Their styles of worship vary, as do their names. For example, you may see nondenominational churches with names such as "Valley Community Church" or "The Little Church in the Vale." Here are examples of marriage vow phrasings commonly used by this type of church.

"Will you have this woman to be your wedded wife, to live together in holy matrimony? Will you love her, comfort her, honor and keep her in sickness and in health, in sorrow and in joy, and, forsaking all others, be faithful to her as long as you both shall live?"

The groom answers:

"I do."

Then, the minister continues by asking the same of the bride.

A very simple form of the traditional Protestant vow is in the form of a statement made by the minister:

> *"This celebration is the outward token of a sacred and inward union of the hearts which the Church does bless and the State makes legal...a union created by loving purpose and kept by abiding will."*

Then the minister asks the bride and groom:

> *"Is it in this spirit and for this purpose that you have come here to be joined together?"*

The bride and groom simply respond:

> *"Yes, I have."*

The couple joins right hands and recites these traditional vows to each other, either from memory, or by prompting from the officiant:

> *"I take you to be my wedded wife / husband,*
> *To have and to hold, from this day forward,*
> *For better, for worse, for richer, for poorer,*
> *In sickness and in health, to love and to cherish,*

Till death do us part.
This is my solemn vow
According to God's holy ordinance;
And thereto I plight you my troth."

♥ ♥ ♥ ♥

"I, _____, take thee, _____,
to be my wedded husband/wife, to have and to
hold, from this day forward, for better, for worse,
for richer, for poorer, in sickness and in health, to
love and to cherish, till death us do part,
according to God's holy ordinance; and thereto I
pledge thee my faith."

♥ ♥ ♥ ♥

Minister (to the groom): "_____, wilt
thou have _____ to be thy wedded
wife, to live together after God's ordinance, in the
holy estate of matrimony? Wilt thou love her,
comfort her, honor, and keep her, in sickness and
in health; and, forsaking all others, keep thee only
unto her, so long as ye both shall live?"

Groom: "I will."

Minister (to the bride): "_____, wilt
thou have _____ to be thy wedded
husband, to live together after God's ordinance, in
the holy estate of matrimony? Wilt thou obey him,
and serve him, love, honor, and keep him, in
sickness and in health; and, forsaking all others,

keep thee only unto him, so long as ye both shall live?"

Bride: "I will."

(The bride and groom join right hands, face each other and repeat the vows after the minister.)

Groom: "I, _____, take thee _____ to be my wedded wife; and I do promise and covenant, before God and these witnesses, to be thy loving and faithful husband, in plenty and in want, in joy and in sorrow, in sickness and in health, as long as we both shall live."

Bride: "I, _____, take thee _____ to be my wedded husband; and I do promise and covenant, before God and these witnesses, to be thy loving and faithful wife, in plenty and in want, in joy and in sorrow, in sickness and in health, as long as we both shall live."

♥ ♥ ♥ ♥

Minister (to the groom): "_____, will you take _____ to be your wedded wife, to live together after God's ordinance in the holy relationship of marriage? Will you love her, comfort her, honor and cherish her in sickness and in health, be true and loyal to her, as long as you both shall live?"

Groom: "I will."

Minister (to the bride): "_____, will you take _____ to be your wedded husband, to live together after God's ordinance in the holy relationship of marriage? Will you love, honor and cherish him in sickness and in health, be true and loyal to him, as long as you both shall live?"

Bride: "I will."

(The bride and groom join right hands, face each other and repeat the vows after the minister.)

Groom: "I, _____, take you _____ to be my wedded wife, to live together after God's ordinance in the holy relationship of marriage. I promise to love and comfort you, honor and keep you, in plenty and in want, in joy and in sorrow, in sickness and in health, and forsaking all others, I will be yours alone as long as we both shall live."

Bride: "I, _____, take you _____ to be my wedded husband, to live together after God's ordinance in the holy relationship of marriage. I promise to love and obey you, honor and keep you, in plenty and in want, in joy and in sorrow, in sickness and in health, and forsaking all others, I will be yours alone as long as we both shall live."

♥ ♥ ♥ ♥

*Minister (to the groom): "_____, will
you take _____ to be your wedded
wife, to live together after God's ordinance in the
holy relationship of marriage? Will you love,
honor and cherish her in sickness and in health,
be true and loyal to her, as long as you both shall
live?"*

Groom: "I will."

*Minister (to the bride): "_____, will
you take _____ to be your wedded
husband, to live together after God's ordinance in
the holy relationship of marriage? Will you love,
honor and cherish him in sickness and in health,
be true and loyal to him, as long as you both shall
live?"*

Bride: "I will."

(The bride and groom join right hands, face each other and
repeat the vows after the minister.)

*Groom: "_____, I now take you to be
my wedded wife, to live together after God's
ordinance in the holy relationship of marriage. I
promise to love and comfort you, honor and keep
you, and forsaking all others, I will be yours
alone as long as we both shall live."*

Bride: "_____, I now take you to be my wedded husband, to live together after God's ordinance in the holy relationship of marriage. I promise to love you and obey you, honor and keep you, and forsaking all others, I will be yours alone as long as we both shall live."

Chapter 2

Nontraditional Vows

The majority of brides and grooms these days are rejecting traditional wedding vows and reciting their own personalized vows instead. The younger the couple, in fact, the less likely they are to subscribe to tradition, particularly strict religious or cultural rules and practices. This disregard for tradition began, as I mentioned in my introduction, back in the 50s and 60s. It was triggered by a number of factors, including an increased number of mixed and ecumenical marriages, which demanded a change in the traditional wording, and the rise of liberated women in society, who rejected any semblance of inequality in male and female roles. Hence, we see revolutionary and fascinating changes in the wording of wedding vows in the 90s. This chapter offers a large selection of these contemporary phrasings.

♥ ♥ ♥ ♥

"_____, we have come here today to celebrate our marriage. A marriage is a commitment between two people, spoken publicly before witnesses. And so, _____, I commit myself to you today, before this congregation of family and friends, without reservation or embarrassment of any kind as I say: I love you; I need you; I thank God for you; and I promise to be a good and faithful husband/wife to you so long as we both shall love."

♥ ♥ ♥ ♥

"I bring myself to you this day to share my life with you; you can trust my love, for it's real. I promise to be a faithful mate and to unfailingly share and support your hopes, dreams and goals. I vow to be there for you always; when you fall, I will catch you; when you cry, I will comfort you; when you laugh, I will share your joy. Everything I am and everything I have is yours, from this moment forth and for eternity."

♥ ♥ ♥ ♥

"Come to me softly, my love; speak to me softly and let me hold your love warm against my heart. May we experience the quiet joys of marriage as our precious love grows deeper through each season. I will be there for you always, holding your hand as we walk together side by side. I give my life to you this day as your loving, devoted husband/wife, and I promise to be faithful and true to you forevermore, from this day forth, through all the adversities and joys of life, as long as God gives us on this earth."

"_____, you are God's precious gift to me, my springtime, my hope and my joy. You are everything that's good and pure and true and I worship you with my mind, body and soul. How blessed I am to be able to say that you are mine, to be able to love and cherish you for the rest of my days. I vow to be a good husband/wife to you, _____, always putting you first in my life, always there to comfort you in your sorrow and rejoice with you in your victories. May our hearts and very breath become one as we unite this day as husband and wife. I promise to be your true love from this day forward and forevermore."

♥ ♥ ♥ ♥

"_____, since you came into my life, my days have been bright and glorious, but today, our wedding day, is the brightest of them all, a golden moment, made splendid by our love for each other. And yet, this beautiful moment is only a taste of what is to come as we share our lives together as husband and wife. I pledge my love to you from this day forward; I promise to be faithful and true to you, rejoicing in my good fortune to have found you as my life-mate."

♥ ♥ ♥ ♥

"_____, I searched for you all my life, looking for you, watching for you, needing you, wanting you, but I didn't know who you were until God finally brought you to me, and your love *touched my heart. You alone are the love of my life, my dream come true. Now that I've found you, I feel that I've known you always, my soul mate, my precious bride / groom. I was only half a person until you came into my life, but now I am whole and complete. How I love and adore you, _____, and I give myself to you this day with complete joy and abandonment; I promise to be a true and faithful husband / wife, to comfort you, honor you and cherish you for all our days together on this earth."*

♥ ♥ ♥ ♥

"_____, this is the most significant moment in my life, the moment I give myself to you as your husband / wife, to join with you in holy matrimony. It is such a miracle to have found you, _____. You have made me completely happy because of my deep assurance of your love for me. There is no question of our devout commitment to each other and I promise to love and cherish you forever as your husband / wife. May this day be just the beginning of an unending joy because of the power of our love."

♥ ♥ ♥ ♥

"The sun smiles on us today, our wedding day, and how can it not, for our love is stronger than forever and our hearts beat together as one. My joy is indescribable as I take you as my husband / wife this day and promise to be a true and faithful husband / wife from this day forward, in all life's

circumstances, as we face them together. In the joys and sorrows, the good times and bad, in sickness or in health, I will always be there for you, to comfort you, love you, honor and cherish you, now and forevermore."

"_____, I vow to be your faithful husband / wife. I offer you my pure and true love and my unwavering support throughout all our lives. As I stand here now, and in the presence of God and these witnesses, I commit myself to you. As we grow and share together, I shall encourage you and strive to help you achieve your full potential as God's creation, then I will celebrate your progress. I give myself to you as I am and as I will be, for all of my life."

"I acknowledge my love for you and invite you to share my life as I hope to share yours. I promise to walk by your side, to love, help and encourage you. I vow to take time to share with you, to listen and to care. I will share your laughter and your tears as your partner, lover and friend. I promise always to respect you and honor you as an individual and to be conscious of your needs. I shall seek through kindness and compassion to achieve with you the life we have planned together."

"Until I met you, marriage-type love was an abstract thing I only read about in poems, heard sung in romantic love songs, or read about in books; but when I met you I knew for the first time what it was to experience this type of love within my heart. You have made me a believer in the real thing, in the promise of a love that will last a lifetime. There is nothing more important to me in my life than your love; I value it above money, power or position. I rejoice in our love, and I promise to walk by your side with a constancy that only comes from unreserved commitment, and it is this commitment I make to you now as I take you as my husband / wife, from this day forward and so long as we both shall live."

"_____, I give myself to you on this, our wedding day, and I promise to be a faithful husband / wife, not only for today, as we celebrate our marriage in this beautiful sanctuary, but as an ongoing commitment, through all the ups and downs of life. I do not expect you to fulfill all my dreams, just as I cannot fulfill all of yours, but I do ask that you share your dreams with me so that I may be your help mate throughout all the years of our lives, and this is my promise."

"It took me a long time to finally find someone I wanted to marry; in fact, my friends used to tease me and said my goals were too high. My goals were high...very high, but they were met when I found you.

I searched for you all my life and, thanks to God, finally found you. You have all the qualities I was hoping to find: You're not only a beautiful person on the outside, but on the inside as well; you're honest, unselfish, loving, caring, supportive, and my ideal woman/man in every way. Yes, my goals were high; but, I have new goals now—to be the faithful, committed husband/wife you deserve. I promise to honor you, respect you, love and cherish you as my husband/wife, from this day forward and until the end of time."

♥ ♥ ♥ ♥

Bride: "_____, *my love for you is eternal.*"

Groom: "_____, *and my love for you is eternal.*"

Bride: "*I give myself to you today as your wife.*"

Groom: "*I give myself to you today as your husband.*"

Bride: "*I promise to love you, honor you, cherish you and respect you, for all the days of our lives.*"

Groom: "*I promise to love you, cherish you, provide for you, and comfort you, for all the days of our lives.*"

Bride: "*We will share our burdens with each other, and so they will seem lighter.*"

Groom: "*We will share our joys together, and so they will be multiplied tenfold.*"

Bride: "*I thank God for you, my precious bridegroom.*"

Groom: "*And I thank God for you, my cherished bride.*"

Bride: "From this day forward I will be faithful to you and always try to be worthy of your love."

Groom: "And I will be faithful to you, also trying to be worthy of your love, from this day forward, so help me God."

Bride: "So help me God."

"_____, you light up my life; before I met you, my days were gray and murky, nondescript, but your love has changed everything. Every day is a superbly happy adventure since I fell in love with you: the rain is softer, the flowers lovelier and a child's laughter more joyous...all because of your love. Thank you for loving me and for lighting up my life with yourself. I am humbled by your love and thankful to be able to return your love from a heart that is spilling over with joy. This is the happiest day of my life as I take you as my husband / wife and commit myself to you for the rest of our lives."

"I take you, _____, this day as my husband / wife, and I promise to walk by your side forever, as your best friend, your lover and your soul mate. You are my beloved one and I am proud to marry you. I promise to support your dreams and to be there for you for all our lives."

"Every experience we have ever had, everything we have ever done, everything we have ever learned, has brought us to this moment when we stand before these witnesses to take each other as husband and wife. As we confront the future together, I promise to stand by your side, as we face new experiences as man and wife, always growing together, honoring, respecting and cherishing each other through all life has in store for us. We bring our individual strengths and weaknesses to this marriage, but as we stand together as a married couple, may we complement each other and be exactly what each other needs as our love and commitment continue to deepen throughout our married life."

"You have filled my world with meaning; you have made me stronger and more fulfilled as a person, and I thank God for bringing you to me. You have made me so happy and my heart rejoices in the anticipation of spending the rest of my life with you. Thank you for taking me as I am, loving me and welcoming me into your heart. I don't deserve such love, but I am eternally grateful. I stand here today before these witnesses and take you as my wife / husband. I promise to return your love in full, as we grow together as man and wife. I promise to always love you, to be faithful to you and to cherish and respect you, in all the circumstances that may come to us in our married life."

"I come to you today just as I am, and I take you just as you are, my cherished husband / wife. Let's never change, but always love each other the way we do today, the man and woman we are as we stand here before these witnesses and commit ourselves to each other for life."

Bride: "I give you my hand in marriage."

Groom: "And I give you mine."

Bride: "Take my hand as a symbol of my love."

Groom: "Take my hand as a symbol of my love."

Bride: "With this hand, I promise to hold you, cherish you and respect you always."

Groom: "With this hand, I promise to care for you, provide for you and to be your friend."

Bride: "As I hold your hand in mine, I feel your love."

Groom: "And I feel your love; our love is not only for this moment, but for a lifetime."

Bride: Yes, for a lifetime."

Up close and personal

I'm a great believer in love at first sight! Especially after six years of interviewing engaged couples and helping them plan their weddings. This is one of those heart-tugging stories: Bill and Kathy Moran met in San Francisco in the summer of 1990 when he was a pharmacy student and she was marketing director for a retail clothing store. Their mutual friend, Mike Moore, had just become engaged and they were both invited to his engagement party; Bill spotted Kathy across the room and immediately asked Mike, "Who is *that*?" When they were introduced, Kathy's first thoughts were: "Wow! What a great guy—cute, outgoing, potentially successful...too bad he lives in Colorado." They were thrown together at a few more social gatherings over that weekend, and as things progressed, they each realized there was a spark between them. When the weekend was over Bill asked Kathy if she would be his official date when he flew back from Colorado for the wedding the following month. Kathy accepted without hesitation and they spent the next four weeks getting to know each other via lengthy telephone conversations.

There was an instant chemistry between them and by the time they met again at Mike's wedding, they both *knew* they had something special. At the wedding everyone else sensed this, as well, and even teased about the "next wedding," referring, of course, to Bill and Kathy. It was so obvious, in fact, that when it came time for Mike to toss the garter, he didn't even bother; he just walked over and *handed* it to Bill.

Kathy rescheduled her business trips over the next four months so that all her flights "just happened" to connect through Denver, allowing them many weekends to get to know each other. A storybook romance unfolded and they became engaged one evening when Bill flew to San Francisco to see her. He took her to her favorite restaurant; then, later that night, with champagne in hand, and on bended knee in the moonlight by the Golden Gate Bridge, he asked her to marry him as he slipped a ring onto her finger. She was so overjoyed that she didn't even look at it. Bill asked her, "Aren't you even going to look at your ring?"

When she glanced down, she saw that it was a "mood" ring and she didn't know what to think. Bill thought that was hilarious, but finally reached back into his pocket for the real thing: a 1-carat diamond solitaire.

They were married in Colorado the following June in a huge white tent in the side courtyard of the Manor House in Ken Caryl Valley. Everything about their wedding was "Cinderella-perfect" until it started to rain and hail, soaking the tent and filling the courtyard with a foot of the white stuff. But it all had a happy ending and here are their personalized vows:

Minister: "William and Kathryn stand before us today to declare their promises openly and gladly. William, will you take Kathryn to be your wedded wife? Will you give yourself to her? Will you share completely with her in your life together? Will you promise to be open and honest in your relationship? Will you give her all comfort and support and strength?"

Bill: "I will."

Minister: "Kathryn, will you take William to be your wedded husband? Will you give yourself to him? Will you share completely with him in your life together? Will you promise to be open and honest in your relationship? Will you give him all comfort and support and strength?"

Kathy: "I will."

Minister: "Kathryn and William, will you now turn and face one another and join hands as you pledge your love and devotion to each other as husband and wife? William, repeat after me:"

Bill (repeating after the minister): "I, William, take you, Kathryn, to be my wife; I promise in the midst of our families and friends and in the presence of God to stand beside and love you always; in times of celebration and times of sadness; in times of pleasure and in times of pain; in times of sickness and times of health; I will be with you and love you as long as we both shall live."

Minister: "Kathryn, repeat after me:"

Kathy (repeating after the minister): "I, Kathryn, take you, William, to be my husband; I promise in the midst of our families and friends and in the presence of God to stand beside and love you always; in times of celebration and times of sadness; in times of pleasure and in times of pain; in times of sickness and times of health; I will be with you and love you as long as we both shall live."

Bill and Kathy honeymooned for two weeks in Florida and the Grand Cayman Islands and now, five years later, they live in Superior, Colorado, with their two beautiful little daughters, Megan Jean and Molly Anne.

"_____, as you know, it is difficult for me to express my feelings in front of others, especially my very private feelings for you. But, here today as I stand in the presence of our family and friends, I want to publicly declare my love for you. And why do I love you so much? I love you because you are the finest person I have ever known; you are unselfish; loving; gentle; loyal; tender; trustworthy; sympathetic; and a joy to be with. Your laughter, your smile and your unfailing optimism buoy me, lift me and make me a

better person. *How can I be so blessed as to be loved by you? What could I have ever done in my lifetime to deserve such a treasure? It is a great mystery. My heart overflows with my love for you and I give myself to you unreservedly today as your faithful husband / wife and I promise to treasure you always, just as I do at this moment."*

"I want you for my husband / wife, to be melded into one as we share our lives together. I want to share my joys with you, and my sorrows, my hopes and my dreams. I promise to walk beside you, to support you, care for you, respect you and cherish you always. You will be first in my life, my most beloved possession. I promise to be faithful to you no matter what the circumstances of life may bring us. I am proud to become your husband / wife."

A rose ceremony

Groom (as he hands his bride a long-stemmed white rose): "_____, take this rose as a symbol of my love. It began as a tiny bud and blossomed, just as my love has grown and blossomed for you."

Bride (as she places the rose into a bud vase filled with water): "I take this rose, a symbol of your love, and I place it into water, a symbol of life. For, just as this rose cannot survive without water, I cannot survive without you."

Groom: "In remembrance of this day, I will give you a white rose each year on our anniversary, as a reaffirmation of my love and the vows spoken here today."

Bride: "And I will refill this vase with water each year, ready to receive your gift, in reaffirmation of the new life you have given me and the vows spoken here today."

Groom (as he and his bride join hands around the rose-filled vase): "And so, this rose will be a symbolic memory of my commitment to you this hour; I vow to be a faithful husband to you, to comfort you, honor you, respect you and cherish you all the days of my life."

Bride (as they continue to hold the vase together): "And I commit myself to you, to be a faithful wife, to comfort you, honor you, respect you and cherish you all the days of my life."

"Today, our wedding day, is one brief day in time, and although our vows are spoken in a matter of minutes, they are promises that will last a lifetime. When we leave this ceremony today, I will be a better person, because of you. Because of your love and trust, my life is fulfilled and has a new beginning. I promise to be a faithful husband and worthy of this love. I will be true and loyal to you in every way, always comforting you, loving you and cherishing you, from this day forward as we begin our new life together."

Bride: "Today is a new beginning."

Groom: "Yes, we leave our pasts behind, and begin a new day."

Bride: "We will be partners."

Groom: "And we will be friends."

Bride: "We will comfort each other."

Groom: "We will honor each other."

Bride: "We will encourage each other."

Groom: "We will uphold each other."

Bride: "I vow to be a good and faithful wife."

Groom: "And I vow to be a good and faithful husband."

Bride: "I want to bear your children, my treasured love."

Groom: "And I want to give them to you, my cherished one."

Bride: "From this day forward, our life is new."

Groom: "Yes, our life is new because of our love."

"_____, it takes a great trust to pledge oneself to another person for a lifetime, and I do that now as I affirm you as my soul mate, my life partner. I promise to mourn with you and to celebrate with you; to love you, honor you, and be faithful to you. I will be your dearest friend, your lover and the

*father / mother of your children. I accept you,
_____, as my husband / wife, and I
pledge myself to you without reservation."*

*Bride: "I promise, before our family and friends, to be
your faithful wife."*

*Groom: "And I promise, before our family and friends,
to be your faithful husband."*

*Bride: "I will do everything in my power to keep our
love as fresh and strong as it is today."*

*Groom: "And I will be true to you, with my body and
my mind, always putting you first in my life."*

*Bride: "Your love has changed my life, and I'm a
better person because of you."*

*Groom: "Your faith in me has given me confidence
and an unexplainable joy."*

*Bride: "I thank God for you and I will love you
always."*

*Groom: "And I will love you always; this is my pledge,
as God is my Witness."*

Bride: "Today is our wedding day."

*Groom: "Yes, today is a sacred day, always to be
remembered."*

Bride: "I come gladly to this moment."

Groom: "And I, too."

Bride: "From this day forward, our lives will be intertwined as one."

Groom: "We will be one flesh."

Bride: "I commit myself to you this day, as your faithful wife."

Groom: "I commit myself to you this day, as your faithful husband."

Bride: "I will nurture you when you need care."

Groom: "I will praise you as you succeed in life."

Bride: "I promise to share my dreams and my fears."

Groom: "I promise to share my hurts and disappointments."

Bride: "I promise to soothe your hurts."

Groom: "And I promise to calm your fears."

Bride: "I promise to be honest with you, never holding back."

Groom: "And I promise to put your needs above mine."

Bride: "I promise to be the best person I can be, so that our life together will be all it should be."

Groom: "And I promise to do everything I can to make you happy for the rest of our lives."

"_____, you are my first love and my last love. Until I met you I didn't give true love much thought, but since you came into my life, I struggle desperately to find the words to tell you how much I love you—how I adore you. It is difficult for me to

verbalize my feelings for you, because mere words
can't begin to express my deep love. I thank God for
you, _____, and I pledge myself to you now,
to be your ever faithful husband/wife. I give you my
body, my mind and my heart and I promise to love
you and cherish you for as long as we both shall live."

"_____, what a great and beautiful
mystery it is for two human souls to join together in
marriage, as I do now join with you and vow to be a
faithful, loving husband/wife, to minister to you in
sorrow, to share with you in gladness and to be one
with you in the silent unspeakable joining of our
hearts. I promise to love you, honor you, comfort you
and cherish you, in sickness and in health, in sorrow
and in joy, from this day forward and forevermore."

Bride: "This is our wedding day."

Groom: "The day we have looked forward to for so
long."

Bride: "I come to you reverently this day, desiring to
be your wife."

Groom: "I come to you reverently this day, desiring to
be your husband."

Bride: "Because of our love, we will be blessed with the
joys and comforts of marriage."

Groom: "Because of our love, we will endure all trials
and cares."

Bride: "I will respect and honor you."

Groom: "I will cherish and protect you."

Bride: "I will be a tender and affectionate wife."

Groom: "I will be a patient and understanding husband."

Bride: "As God is my witness, I commit myself to you for all the days of our lives."

Groom: "As God is my witness, I commit myself to you for all the days of our lives."

Bride: "From this day forward, and forevermore."

Groom: "From this day forward, and forevermore."

"_____, I love you and I want to be your husband/wife. I promise to be a patient husband/ wife, always honest and compassionate. I will be your best friend, your sweetheart, your helpmate throughout life, always putting you first above my own needs. And I promise to live a life that will honor the vows we have spoken and make you glad to have married me this day."

"_____, I take you as my husband/wife. You are my once-in-a-lifetime, my miracle. May our lives intermingle and our love grow as we become one. You are all I could ever need in my life...my friend...my lover...my everything. I promise to be faithful to you, to love you, honor you, live with you

and cherish you, according to the commandments of God, in the holy bond of marriage."

♥ ♥ ♥ ♥

Up close and personal

Here's a very 90s story of Eric Wood and Kimberly Gray who met at a country western dance bar by the name of Cactus Jack's. She is a clerk at a coffee bar at Gelson's Markets in Newport Beach, California, and Eric works as a senior dock worker for Viking Freight Systems. He hopes to transfer to their communications department after he graduates from ITT Tech in May of 1996. The night they met at Cactus Jack's, Kimberly bravely invited him to go to the movies with her and some friends; the sparks flew and as Kimberly says, their relationship "just fell into place" and within two weeks they "knew it was forever" and they are now engaged to be married.

Their wedding will have a country western theme with the men wearing jet black jeans, black boots, cowboy hats and country cut vests with prairie ties. Kimberly's wedding gown is being created by her grandmother from a pattern they found in the Harper House Past Patterns catalog; she's going to wear white boots, a floral tiara and her hair in a Gibson Girl bun. The judge who will marry them has agreed to wear traditional parson's attire.

Eric and Kimmie, as she is called, have written their own vows for their wedding and have graciously agreed to share them with us; the vows will be integrated with a Unity Candle ceremony.

*Eric (to Kimberly) and Kimberly (to Eric): "I,
Kimberly Joy / Eric Kevin, take you, Eric
Kevin / Kimberly Joy, to be my lawfully wedded
husband / wife. I promise before our families,
friends, and the Lord, to care for you in sickness
and in sadness and I promise to laugh with you
and rejoice with you in gladness. I promise to
inspire greatness in you and to listen and give to
you from my heart and soul. I make this vow in
love, keep it in faith, live it in hope, and share it in
honesty, as long as our souls shall live."*

(These vows will be followed by the Unity Candle Ceremony which consists of the lighting of a central candle from two separate candles held by the bride and groom to symbolize the uniting of two lives into one. Their wedding vows will be inscribed on the large unity candle. In the years to come, on each wedding anniversary, they will reaffirm these vows as they again light the candle in celebration.)

Kim and Eric have also composed beautifully worded ring vows; look for them in Chapter 8.

♥ ♥ ♥ ♥

*Groom: "I love you _____, and I promise
to be a loving and caring husband. I promise to
always cherish your presence and place our
marriage above all else."*

*Bride: "I love you _____, and I promise
to always be there for you. I promise to receive your
love with love and to work hard at keeping our
marriage true and everlasting."*

♥ ♥ ♥ ♥

"You are my love, my life, my very breath. Until you came to me, I was searching for you, longing for you. Today we become one flesh as we unite in holy matrimony, a sacred commitment to share our lives together and to be true to each other as long as we both shall live. I promise to give you the best of myself, to respect you as your own person, to bring joy, strength and imagination to our relationship. I will be your true and faithful wife / husband, and this is my solemn vow to you this day, _____, so help me God."

♥ ♥ ♥ ♥

"_____, we have chosen each other as life partners and today is our wedding day. As we enter this new world of marital bliss, I promise to share all that I am and all that I have—not just my home and my material possessions, but my inner world, my feelings, concerns, values, joys, hopes and dreams. I also promise to share your hurts, tears and failures, as if they were my very own. I will bond to you in love, devote myself to you and strive to make you happy for all the days of my life."

♥ ♥ ♥ ♥

"_____, today I choose you to be my life partner, and I do it proudly and openly in the presence of these witnesses. I promise to love you always, to listen to you, to nourish you with my

praise, to never take you for granted, to hold you close when you need to be held, to laugh with you when you laugh and to always be your safe haven in this life. I will be faithful to you, even as we grow old together and our bodies age, even when we face illness, and even if we should have financial problems. I will love you truly and joyfully from this moment on, and I promise this from my heart, with my soul and until death parts us."

♥ ♥ ♥ ♥

"Today I choose you, _____, to be my life partner. I promise to sleep by your side, to be the joy of your heart, the food to your soul and the best person I can be for you. I promise to laugh with you when times are good, and to suffer with you when they are bad; I promise to wash away your tears with my kisses and to hold you sweetly and gladly until our days on earth are over."

♥ ♥ ♥ ♥

"I take you, _____, as my adored and cherished wife / husband and I promise to be a loving and faithful husband / wife. May our sunshine be shared, our rains be gentle and our sweet love eternal. I pledge myself to you from this day forward and for all eternity."

♥ ♥ ♥ ♥

"_____, I consider it an honor and a privilege to be the one you have chosen as your life's mate. I promise to be a true and faithful husband/wife, to love you, respect you and be honest with you always. I promise to be supportive of your goals and as you grow intellectually, emotionally and spiritually, I will be by your side rooting for you all the way. Never be afraid to confide in me...I promise to be a good listener and a safe confidant. You are always welcome into my innermost world, and I promise to share my goals and ideas with you. As we grow together throughout our marriage, there are no limitations on the possibilities of our relationship and I hope we never realize just how high our high can be. I believe in you, _____, and I will be there for you always."

♥ ♥ ♥ ♥

"I, _____, in the name of God, take you, _____, to be my husband/wife, from this time onward, to join with you and to share with you all that is to come, to give and to receive, to speak and to listen, to inspire and to respond, and in all our life together to be loyal and to cherish you with my whole being, as long as we both shall live."

♥ ♥ ♥ ♥

"_____, I want you to be my wife/husband, not only for the good days, the warm sunny days, but for the dark days, as well, when it's cold and rainy. May we survive every season and every storm, until there is no more life. I want you to live with me; I *want to share your thoughts, your hopes, your dreams. I want you to be my lover, my friend, the mother/father of my children, the heart of our home, and I will stand by your side for all the days of my life. I love you _____."*

♥ ♥ ♥ ♥

"I, _____, take you, _____, to be my wife/husband, and I commit myself to you. I promise to be responsible in our marriage relationship and to give myself to you in every way. I invite you fully into my being so that I may know who you are, the better to cherish you above all things and to respect your individuality by always encouraging you to be yourself. I promise to forsake all others and to be faithful to you as long as we both shall live."

♥ ♥ ♥ ♥

"_____, my beloved, I offer myself to you today as your husband/wife. I offer everything I am, everything I have, everything I hope to be. I present to you everything that is broken in me, for your touch, your mending, your healing balm of love, and it is my desire, also, to be your healer and nurturer. I entrust myself to your heart on this, our sacred wedding day, and for tomorrow, and for all the days of our lives."

♥ ♥ ♥ ♥

"_____, you are a kind and gentle man/woman, and it is with great joy that I take

you as my wife/husband; may our love grow deeper every day of our marriage, and as the days grow to weeks, and the weeks to months, and the months to years, may we never forget this joyous day and the vows of commitment we are pledging to each other. I will cherish you and be faithful to you for all eternity."

"_____, I take you this day as my cherished wife/husband. You are all I ever dreamed of, or dared to hope for—only God could have given me such a gift. I choose to marry you this day and I want to grow old with you. You are the joy of my life, the love of my heart and my reason for living. I commit myself to you for all eternity."

Special occasion vows
Valentine's Day:

"It is fitting that we marry on Valentine's Day, the most romantic day of the year, when lovers celebrate their love; truly, we celebrate our love today as our hearts are joined in holy, sacred matrimony. I will hold gently the heart you have given me this day, a lasting treasure to be cherished, and I give my heart to you with joy and abandonment, as I promise to be your faithful husband/wife. Every year we will reaffirm our vows on Valentine's Day, as we celebrate our wedding day, the day we gave our hearts to each other until the end of time."

"I give my heart to you completely as your husband / wife; from this moment on it will always be with you. There will be no escape from my love. If you fly away, I will fly after you. If you walk down a secret path, I will follow you. If you sail away to the farthest corner of the earth, I will find you, because you are mine; you belong to me. And if you should fall, I will lift you up; if you should feel weak, I will cover you with my strength. From this day forward, you are in my heart and I am in yours; our hearts are intertwined and nothing will ever separate us."

New Year's Eve or Day:

"As we put the past behind us and embark on a new year, so we put our individual lives behind us as we become one in holy matrimony. And just as a new year is bright and promising, so you are my new day, my hope, my joy and the sunshine of our future together. Take my hand (takes bride's / groom's hand) and walk with me into the new year and into our new life as my husband / wife. I give you my heart and everything that I am as we begin our lives together, united as one flesh."

Christmas Eve or Day:

"Christmas is the birthday of Jesus Christ, God's sacrificial gift to us, and so we have come to marry on this sacred day and give ourselves to each other in the spirit of Christmas, with a holy, sacrificial love for

*each other. On this silent night / sacred day, I give
myself to you, _____, as your loving,
faithful husband / wife as I offer my gift of love to you,
a gift that shall endure until the end of time. Every
year of our lives, as we gather during the Christmas
season and give gifts to each other, I promise to give
myself anew to you in remembrance and honor of the
vows we are taking here today."*

Garden or forest wedding

*"As we stand in the shade of God's creation, I offer
myself to you as your husband / wife. Our love is
reflected in the flower's blooms and the strength of the
towering trees, always growing, always searching for
perfection, just as the trees reach for the heavens and
the blooms open their faces to the sun. Just as this
garden / forest is a living thing, so may our union
continue always to thrive until death do part us from
His earth."*

*"As we stand in this garden among the flowers of
God's creation, I offer you the flower of my heart as my
wedding gift to you. This flower is pure and innocent;
beautiful and eternal. It needs the care and
nourishment that only you can give it. Place this
flower within your own heart; love it; keep it safe; and
give it light; and may it bloom forever from this day
forward as I commit it to you with my eternal love as
your wife / husband."*

(The bride and groom may actually hand a flower to each
other as he or she recites this vow.)

Seaside wedding

"As we stand beside the ocean tide, may our love always be as constant and unchanging as these never-ending waves that pour beneath our feet, flowing endlessly from the depths of the sea; your love came softly upon my heart, just as the foam comes softly upon the sand, and just as there will never be a morning without the ocean's flow, so there will never be a day without my love for you. I pledge myself to you this day and I promise to be your faithful husband / wife, as unchanging and dependable as the tide; as these waters nourish the earth and sustain life, may my constant love nourish and sustain you until the end of time."

"As the sea is eternal, so is our love; as the wind is all-encompassing, so is our love; as the earth is solid beneath our feet, so is our love. And yet, our love is so great that it even soars beyond the sea and the wind and the earth. It is so perfect to be standing beside you here, among these elements which reflect the love we have for each other. Every year on our anniversary, we will come here, to stand on this very spot, as we commit ourselves to each other anew, just as I commit myself to you this day."

Vows for those who were childhood sweethearts

"_____, *we have known each other
since childhood when we played together in my back
yard, making pancakes in the sandbox and swinging
each other high on the rope swing that Dad hung in
the apple tree. We were in preschool together at Mrs.
Meredith's, and elementary school, too. Then, in
junior high and high school, we spent many hours
together as we studied for exams and attended the
games and the school dances. When was it we fell in
love? When we were 18? Or, 16? Or, maybe when we
were 10...for it seems that I have always been in love
with you, and I've always wanted you to be my
husband / wife. And now, today, we stand here, in the
presence of our family and friends, and commit
ourselves to each other, to be faithful and true to each
other for the rest of our lives. I love you,
_____, and I am so thankful we met at
such a young age and that our friendship grew into a
deep marriage-type love. I commit myself to you this
day, _____, and I promise to be your
faithful husband / wife, to love and cherish you, in
sickness or in health, in good times or bad, for richer
or poorer, from this day forward and forevermore.*"

"*Remember when we were children and we used to
dress up and pretend we were bride and groom? Those
were days of playful childish fantasies, but today is for
keeps. Today you are a real bride / groom, and I am a
real groom / bride...no more childishness...no more
games of pretend. Today, as I give myself to you as
your bride / husband, my mind is clear and my
commitment is strong and without reservation as I*

take you to be my life's partner. I will never leave you nor forsake you; I will spend all my days at your side, and leaving behind childish things, we will share a lifetime of eternal, immeasurable love."

(Customize your vows to include how you met and your own childhood memories.)

"Today is the most important day of our lives, the day we put our individual pasts behind us and go forward into the future as one. We have thousands of memories of our past: our childhoods, our growings-up, the day we met, the day we knew we were meant to be. But today is the first day of the rest of our lives and we will build new memories together. There will be no more you; and no more me; but only us, from this moment on. I promise to try, with God's help, to be the best husband / wife I can be, so that our memories will be treasures for all the years to come."

Chapter 3

Vows for Second Marriages

There is almost always a great deal of heartache when a first marriage dissolves, whether by death or divorce. The estranged man or woman is usually convinced he or she will never be the same again. Yet as time passes, wounds heal, and the individual finds someone special with whom to share his or her life. This is why most couples feel compelled to write their own personalized vows for a second marriage—vows that encompass their special needs and feelings. I hope you find the words to express the feelings of your own hearts as you read these poignant, meaningful vows, written by brides and grooms who married again.

♥ ♥ ♥ ♥

"_____, you are my new day, a
beautiful ray of light that broke through the darkness
of my despair. I thank God for sending you to me with
your smile, your sense of humor and your loving
spirit. I take you today as my wedded wife / husband,
and I promise to love you and cherish you all the days
of my life."

♥ ♥ ♥ ♥

"_____, you are my healer, my
comforter, and the joy of my life. Your love has
restored my torn, broken heart; your smile has healed
my pain; and your caring spirit has rescued mine
from the dark places. I love you, _____, and I
vow to be a faithful, loving husband / wife, to care for
you, to comfort you and to cherish you for as long as
we both shall live."

♥ ♥ ♥ ♥

"I, _____, take you,
_____, as my lawfully wedded
husband / wife. I promise to love you and be true to
you in sickness and in health, in good times and bad,
always putting you first in my life. I thank God for
rescuing me from my despair by sending you to me,
my cherished treasure, His most precious, undeserved
gift."

♥ ♥ ♥ ♥

"_____, I thank God for you and for the
joyous light and peace you have brought to me at a

dark time in my life. *With a love that will never falter
and our abiding faith in one another, I vow to take
you, _____, as my husband / wife, to love
you, honor you and cherish you now and forevermore,
so help me God."*

♥ ♥ ♥ ♥

*"God sent you to me, _____, as a precious
gift, to heal my broken heart. You have brought
sunshine to my soul, joy to my days, and love to my
life. I thank God for you and I take you this day as my
husband / wife. May every day of our lives be full of an
awareness of our existence for each other. My heart is
open and my soul rejoices this day as we become one."*

♥ ♥ ♥ ♥

*"_____, you are the sunshine of my life
after the storms, my sweet nectar after the bitterness of
my days, and my joy after the painful seasons of
sorrow. I will love you always and forever, my
Godsend, my sweet husband / wife, my miracle healer,
my lover, my friend. What grace God bestowed when
He gave you to me, and I come to you today joyfully
and without reservation, to take you as my lawfully
wedded husband / wife, to hold and cherish
forevermore. I promise to be faithful to you and to care
for you in all circumstances of life, in good times and
in bad, in joy and in sorrow, in sickness and in
health, so help me God."*

♥ ♥ ♥ ♥

Up close and personal

Kathy Welch, a single mother of two children, was reasonably happy with her life in Belmar, New Jersey. She says, "I had been divorced for four years and the last thing I ever wanted was to get remarried. I had made a pretty good life for myself and my children, working as a logistician/secretary for an Army hospital, and although money was really tight, we didn't think we were missing anything. The three of us were very happy. That is...until Joe came along!"

Kathy met Joe McLaughlin, a divorced father, through her children's Cub Scout and Little League baseball activities. They were friends for over a year before Joe finally asked her on an official "first date"; he was being honored at a Boy Scout dinner and asked if she wanted to go with him. After a year of dating, he proposed in a unique way: They had attended his secretary's wedding and stopped at his home between the ceremony and the reception; he asked Kathy to sit down in a swivel chair and close her eyes, which she did. Then, he spun her around and told her to open her eyes to see a huge banner on the wall that read, "Kathy, will you marry me?" He was down on his knees by this time and Kathy started to cry. Of course, she said yes.

Although Joe was a construction inspector/engineering technician, he was also a volunteer fireman, so their wedding had a fireman motif, from the reception to the bride/fireman wedding cake topper, to the little fireman hat place cards, to their wedding invitations and ceremony programs.

Their invitations read like this:

Please join

Kathleen Mary Boyd Welch

and

Joseph Henry McLaughlin

as they take two flames

and

make them one

Friday, the ninth of June

Nineteen hundred and ninety-five

at six o'clock in the evening

Saint James Episcopal Church

605 Fourth Avenue

Bradley Beach, New Jersey

Their ceremony programs incorporated fire-related words from the Song of Solomon in the Bible:

Love bursts into flame and burns

like a raging fire

Water cannot put it out;

No flood can drown it.

Kathy says of their vows, "We knew our wedding had to be more personalized than our first ones had been. We knew that the traditional vows were nice, but we needed to say something more personal." And so, they wrote these beautifully worded vows, although the opening was borrowed. from a traditional Jewish veil-lifting ceremony:

"O God, who has ordained marriage as the sanctification of the love of man and woman, I turn to Thee in prayer at this solemn moment. I thank Thee for him / her who is about to become my husband / wife and for our love for each other. Enable me to be a worthy wife / husband unto her / him. Grant that our marriage be marked by happiness and mutual devotion.

"Joe / Kathy, these words come from my heart with all my love; with everything I am and everything I have. I love you for what you are to me and what you are to others.

"I will be your wife / husband and your friend, showing pride as both. I will love you when we are together and when we are apart: to stand beside you through life's good times and bad; through sickness and health. I will show compassion when you are sad and joy when you are happy. I will encourage and support all your endeavors. I will give you honesty and sincerity. And I will accept and love your family as my own.

"I give my love, my soul, myself, only to you, starting today, until we are separated by God.

"Joe / Kathy, I give you this ring with all that I have and with all that I am. It represents my love for you and as that, it shows no beginning and no end. I ask that you wear it as an outward symbol of my love and that it may remind you and to show others, how much you mean to me."

By the way, their children served as their attendants and had a very important part in the ceremony.

"_____, your smile is a tonic to my battered soul, a healer of my broken heart, a blessing beyond description. How thankful I am to have found you at last, my soul mate, my other half. As we become one flesh today, I am overwhelmed by my love for you. I adore you, _____, and I worship you with my body, mind and spirit. I pledge, with God's help, to be a good and faithful husband / wife, always tender in my feelings toward you, always caring and devoted, always true to you throughout all circumstances of life, from this day on and forevermore."

"As we begin our new life together as husband and wife, I am amazed at our love. It is an invisible thing—our love—and yet, it is a force so strong, so durable that it will hold our lives together for all the years to come. Our past is over; our future is new, and as we take our vows today, we will be changed forever, and I take them gladly, and without reservation. _____, I commit myself to you, to be your loving, faithful husband / wife. I promise to honor you, believe in you, protect you and do everything in my power to make your life happy and fulfilled. This is my promise. Take my hand as we go with joy into our new life together."

"_____, when God brought you into my life, everything changed. Because of you, I laugh, I smile, I dare to dream again. All the heartaches and sorrows are behind me now, and by God's grace, and because of you, I look forward with great joy to spending the rest of my life with you, caring for you, nurturing you, being there for you in all life has for us, and I vow to be a true and faithful husband/wife, for as long as we both shall live, so help me God."

"From your first hello on the day we met, there was fresh meaning to my life. You came to me and you were mine from that first moment, brought to me by God's grace, just in time to rescue me from my empty world. You've filled my heart with your love and as we marry this day, my life is finally complete. I know that for the rest of my days you'll always be there for me, and I for you. My love for you cannot be measured and I promise to devote the rest of my life to you, as a tender and faithful husband/wife, always putting you first, caring for you, and loving you through all the ups and downs of life from this day forward."

"_____, God has given us a second chance at happiness and I praise Him for that. I come today to give you my love, to give you my heart and my hope for our future together. I promise to bring you joy, to be at home with your spirit and to learn to love you more each day, through all the days of our lives. I promise to be your faithful wife/husband; my love for you is seamless, endless and eternal."

"When I first met you, _____, I was
drawn to you immediately, but I was resigned never to
marry again, after the pain I had suffered through the
years. But your love was so tender and genuine, so
compassionate and caring, until you crept slowly into
my life; inch by inch you permeated my being, as your
love fell softly onto my heart and I became addicted to
your love. You have turned my life around; it will
never be the same. Because of your love, each day is a
new delight, a new awakening. My heart belongs to
you, dear _____, and I pledge here today,
in the presence of these witnesses, to be your faithful
husband / wife, to stand beside you, upholding you,
cherishing you for the rest of our lives."

♥ ♥ ♥ ♥

"_____, I am proud to marry you this
day and become your husband / wife. I promise to
wipe away your tears with my laughter, and your
pain with my caring and my compassion. We will
wipe out the old canvases of our lives and let God,
with His amazing artistic talent, fill them with new
color, harmony and beauty. I give myself to you
completely as your husband / wife and I promise to
love you always, from this day forth."

♥ ♥ ♥ ♥

"_____, we are blessed beyond measure
this day as we stand here, bound by our eternal love.
How I thank God for bringing you to me, my beloved,
as a healer to my soul and as a hope for my future. I
promise to be faithful to you, to honor you, to grow

with you through the years, to suffer with you, to rejoice with you. Because I have never known such a love as this before, I take you now and forever as my dear husband / wife."

♥ ♥ ♥ ♥

"Today I have come to marry my best friend, my life-saver, my sweetheart. Before I met you, I was only half a person, a broken man / woman, filled with sadness and regret. But your love has made me whole again. Together we will face life with gladness and thanksgiving, welcoming all God's blessings in store for us. I am humbled by your love, and I will stay with you, in love, for all of our days. I accept you as my husband / wife; will you accept me as your husband / wife?"

♥ ♥ ♥ ♥

Up close and personal

I would like to close this chapter by telling you another true story of a couple I know; I'll call them Bill and Anna, to protect their identities. Bill and Anna lived two doors apart in a Northern California suburb when they were growing up and they, along with all their blond-haired, blue-eyed, Scandinavian brothers and sisters, played together every day. By the time Bill and Anna were in junior high school they were sweethearts and never dated anyone else until after their high school graduation. It was then that Bill went away to college and met, fell in love with, became engaged to and married a stunning Mexican-American girl with glorious waist-length black hair. Meanwhile, Anna met and married a tall, handsome Italian man and a year later gave birth to a baby boy.

After they had been married for about five years they were each divorced. Bill's wife left him one day while he was at work, after loading up most of their material goods and cleaning out both of their bank accounts, leaving this note: "Bill—I don't love you anymore. I never loved you. I'm leaving you." Bill was, of course, shocked and devastated. Meanwhile, Anna discovered that her handsome, fun-loving husband was doing and dealing drugs, which led to heated arguments between them and their last day together was the day he physically abused her.

Bill and Anna each moved back home with their families and eventually began seeing each other, first as friends trying to comfort each other through the grief. Eventually—you guessed it—they realized how much they loved each other and had always loved each other, as a matter of fact.

They were married in a beautiful garden wedding as they stood before the minister with Anna's son between them, each of them holding one of his hands. It was one of the most poignant, emotional, tearful weddings ever witnessed as these two incredibly beautiful people became husband and wife. Here are the touching vows they wrote for their wedding:

> *Bill: "Anna, mere words cannot express my love for you, my need for you, my joy in finding you after suffering such heartache and grief. I have been stumbling around this earth, only half a man, with a dark, gaping hole in my heart, but your love has filled that void completely, and I am whole again. As we become one flesh on this our wedding day, I vow to be*

*a loving, faithful husband, always rejoicing in you
and praising God for you, until death do us part."*

*Anna: "Bill, our God and Savior, the healer of broken
hearts, has rescued us in His perfect time, and has
given us to each other to love and to cherish for all the
days of our lives. I promise to love and honor you, in
all faith and tenderness, to live with you according to
the ordinance of God, in the holy, sacred bond of
marriage."*

I love happy endings. Don't you?

Chapter 4

Vows That Include Children

It has become quite natural for the children of the bride or groom to be included in the wedding service, serving as attendants or participants in the service itself. It is felt that by bringing a child into the wedding experience and helping him feel an integral part of it, the easier it will be for him to accept his new mommy or daddy and to feel part of the new family being created at this ceremony. Here are the ways several couples have included their children in their weddings.

♥ ♥ ♥ ♥

Minister (addressing the groom—referring to the child): "And do you, _____, take _____ as your own, promising to love her and care for her, providing for her needs, physical and spiritual?"

Groom: "I do."

Minister (addressing the child): "And do you, _____, take _____, to be your loving father from this day forward?"

The child: "I do."

Groom (addressing the child): "_____, I place this ring on your finger as a sign of my loving promise made this day."

♥ ♥ ♥ ♥

Groom (addressing his bride): "I love you, _____, and I love your children as my very own. My joy is multiplied tenfold because of _____ and _____. Their love fills a void in my life, a place that has remained empty for all of these years; filled now with their innocent sweetness and trusting devotion, I am complete at last. And so, we are a family and I am blessed beyond belief as I marry you this day, my precious one, my Godsend. I vow to be a true and faithful husband / wife to you, in sickness or in health, in joy or in sorrow, in good times or in bad, from this day forward and forevermore, and I don't take my responsibilities as a father lightly, but with great gravity and sincerity. I vow to be a faithful, loving, tender and nurturing father / mother as well, always there for _____ and _____, not only providing their physical needs, but their emotional needs as well, always a good listener, a loving counselor and a friend."

♥ ♥ ♥ ♥

"Because of you, my heart is at peace at last; because of you, I am happy and stable; because of you, I look forward to the future with joy instead of dread; because of you, my world is whole again; because of you, I believe in marriage anew; and because of you, my children will be blessed with a loving mother / father. You are the kindest, gentlest, most loving person I have ever met; what a blessing that I met you that day after church (personalize this to meet your circumstances) and that our friendship grew into a love that is eternal. I commit myself to you this day as your husband / wife and as the mother / father of your children. May God bless our marriage and our new family."

♥ ♥ ♥ ♥

Up close and personal

This is a true story that is very dear to my heart because it is the love story of my son and the woman he married almost two years ago. Darren was a 29-year-old attorney when he met Lisa, and by that time my husband and I were beginning to wonder if he would ever find someone who would meet his high standards.

One summer Sunday afternoon when Darren was playing his trombone with a Sacramento jazz band at a charity concert, he noticed a stunning woman in the audience and he couldn't take his eyes off of her. There was quite a crowd there that day and she disappeared after the concert before he could come up with a way to meet her, although he did ask around to see if anyone knew who she was. Finally, two months later his band was playing for another fund raiser when he saw her again in the audience, and this time he wheedled an introduction. She told Darren immediately about her recent divorce and her young son, expecting Darren to lose interest. He didn't, however, and although she refused to give him her telephone number, he finally convinced her to take his telephone number and give him a call sometime.

After an agonizing week of waiting, Darren finally heard from her and the two of them hit it off immediately over the phone. After a week of telephone conversations, they agreed to meet at a restaurant for dinner, which became their first date.

Slowly, but surely, they got to know each other, fell in love and were eventually married at The Lodge at Pebble Beach in Carmel on an elevated terrace overlooking the ocean and the 18th green. Lisa's son, Jeffrey, was 3 years old at the time of the wedding, and this is the vow Darren wrote and recited to him that day as Darren knelt down and placed an arm around Jeffrey who stood sweetly and quietly in his miniature black tuxedo:

> *"Jeffrey, I promise to be there as a father to you, to protect you, to support and comfort you and our family, and to love you all the days of my life."*

I usually do a pretty good job of keeping my emotions under control during a wedding, but this was one time I lost it completely and couldn't stop the flow of tears. In fact, both my husband and I had a tough time controlling our emotions because of the joy we felt for all three of them. We were so happy for Darren to have finally found Lisa, such a beautiful person inside and out, but to also have little Jeffrey as part of his instant family was almost more joy than our hearts could bear.

"Not only do I vow to be a good and faithful husband to you, _____, but I also vow to be a patient, loving father to _____, _____ and _____, caring for them and providing for them as my own. I vow to be their strength and their emotional support, loving them with all my heart from this day forward."

"As we become one on this, our wedding day, we become part of each other: your feelings become my feelings; your sorrows become my sorrows; your joys become my joys; your worries become my worries, and your children become my children. I promise to be a true and faithful husband / wife and father / mother, always there to comfort you, rejoice with you and endure all the complexities of life that we will face together as a family in the years to come. My love for you and the children is pure and unshakable and I hereby commit myself to all of you from this day forth and forevermore."

In a recent wedding on a yacht anchored at a marina on Orcas Island in the San Juans, a couple recited their vows. The bride stood with her two children at her side. When the minister asked her:

"Do you take this man?"

she turned to her two children, bent down, talked to them privately for a moment, and then, finally, turned back to the minister and said:

"I do."

This small gesture gave her children a feeling of being included in her vows.

♥ ♥ ♥ ♥

"I have promised to love you and to be a faithful husband / wife, but I would like to add another vow, a promise to love _____ as my own child, to provide for him / her and to be a faithful father / mother, always concerned for his / her welfare and his / her every need."

♥ ♥ ♥ ♥

"_____, did you know that you are a little bit of heaven to me? Although the golden days of childhood come and go so quickly, I promise that I will always be there for you. I love you dearly and I promise to be a faithful father to you for all the days of my life."

♥ ♥ ♥ ♥

Vow to a new stepdaughter

"_____, I love your Mommy, and today I have taken her as my wife; but, did you know that I love you dearly as well? I want to be as a father to you, and I invite you into my heart. We will have happy times together, you and your Mommy and I. And with this ring I give you my love." (Slides the ring onto the girl's finger.)

♥ ♥ ♥ ♥

Up close and personal

Another beautiful love story involves the bride's daughter from her previous marriage. Ben King, currently a cattle rancher, and Wendi Moore-James, a pharmacy technician, met at California State University, Stanislaus during the fall semester of 1993. They were friends for several months before they started dating, but after dating for about six months, Wendi's 3-year-old daughter, Cheyenne, began calling Ben "Daddy," completely on her own, without any prompting. When Ben and Wendi were married on September 16, 1995 in Hilmar, California, following their traditional vows, the minister asked Cheyenne, who served as a flower girl and was standing a few feet away, to come stand beside Ben. Then these words were spoken:

> *Minister: "Ben, do you wish to receive Cheyenne as your daughter?"*
>
> *Ben: "I do."*
>
> *Minister: "Do you promise to love her, raise her, guide her, teach her and be a father to her?"*
>
> *Ben: "I do."*
>
> *Minister: "Do you have something you would like to give her?"*
>
> *Ben: "Yes."*

(Ben took a tiny heart-shaped ring with a center diamond from his pocket, knelt down and placed the ring on Cheyenne's finger, followed by a hug and a kiss.)

At the end, the minister introduced the couple to the congregation as "Mr. and Mrs. King and daughter, Cheyenne."

Ben loves and adores Cheyenne as much as he would if they were biologically related, and Cheyenne tells people that "she's married to Ben." She didn't think it was fair, however, that she couldn't go on the honeymoon!

Children included in congregational blessing

Children are often included as part of the congregational blessing upon the bride, groom and their child or children.

Minister to the congregation: "Will you lend your hearts and concerns to this couple and their children, upholding them in prayer and encouraging them in their new life together?"

The congregation responds: "We will."

As I close this chapter, I have one more little story. A friend of mine took a Caribbean cruise recently and witnessed a poolside wedding. The bride and groom evidently brought their families along for the wedding and the bride's teenaged daughter served as her maid of honor. During the ring ceremony, after the groom had recited his ring vows and placed a wedding ring on his bride's finger, he unexpectedly reached inside his pocket and pulled out a delicate gold-banded birthstone ring, which he placed on the finger of the bride's daughter, symbolizing her inclusion in the marriage.

Isn't it a lovely new trend to include the children in the ceremony? I think so.

Chapter 5

Reaffirmation Vows

A reaffirmation ceremony is a time of thanksgiving and assessment of a couple's years together. It is also a strengthening of their commitment to each other. By the time a couple has been married 10, 25, 40 or 50 years, they have successfully survived a myriad of crises in their lives through their deep love for each other and their reaffirmation vows may be personalized to reflect this. Or a couple may prefer to duplicate their original wedding ceremony as closely as possible, including the original minister, if he is still available. The members of the original wedding party are often included as well, along with the couple's newly extended family of children, grandchildren, nieces and nephews.

Many families create exhibits and displays honoring the couple, including photographs taken on their wedding day, the original wedding certificate, a photograph of their first home, family snapshots and scrapbooks, a photo montage of the couple and all their family members, their original wedding album, plus a sentimental item or two unique to their life together, such as a cradle he may have made by hand for their first baby, etc.

A very simple way to handle the vows in a reaffirmation ceremony is for the minister to read the actual vows that were made at the couple's wedding ceremony, then ask the couple if they do freely reaffirm those vows right at that moment. The minister may ask, after reading their original vows:

> *"Remembering these vows, made so many years ago on _____ 19_____, do you now reaffirm these vows and your love for each other?"*
>
> *The couple answers: "I do."*

However, for those couples who would like to personalize their reaffirmation vows, this chapter offers many touching choices.

> *"I thank God, our Father, for bringing us together to love and care for each other. Every year, as we have walked through our days together, whether joyous or difficult, I thanked God to have you by my side. You have always been there for me, _____, filled with love, understanding and encouragement, freely offering a smile and a hug. Today, as we reaffirm our wedding vows, I commit my life to you anew and I vow to be a loving, true and faithful husband as long as we both shall live."*

"_____, ours has been a fairy tale love story...from that first day we met until this very moment, our love has been one to be envied. We have been partners who grew more and more in love each day as we journeyed through life together. Our children have been the fruit of our love, and our grandchildren as well. We have a lifetime of shared memories, shared joys, shared sorrows, and our love has soared above it all. Today, as we renew our wedding vows before our beloved friends and family, I do so as an expression of how much I love and adore you. Ours is a love story destined to continue until death do us part."

"As we stand here today renewing our wedding vows, I recall our wedding day so well. We were so young, so hopeful, so full of dreams. And most of our dreams have come true...but not all. And the disappointments hurt more than we thought they would, didn't they? And yet, our good times together were even better than we expected. If I could have known then what I know now, would I have married you? Oh, yes, most certainly—and with the same joy and commitment I feel today as I promise to be your devoted and faithful husband / wife for whatever years we have left in this life."

Up close and personal

It was another one of those high school sweetheart things. She was a cheerleader and one of the prettiest girls in the school, and he was the quarterback of the football team and popular with everyone on campus. Because this couple has asked to remain anonymous, I will call them Jim and Mary. Mary was two years younger than Jim, so he graduated and was off to college ahead of her. Their relationship held, however, as their tender love letters flew back and forth and he drove home to see her on weekends as often as he could; that is, if he could get his old Plymouth up and running.

Mary graduated from high school in June of 1955 and they were married that August. They moved into a married couples' dorm at Jim's university and he finally graduated with a B.A. in psychology that he had planned to use in a teaching career. After his graduation, however, their future took an abrupt turn as they accepted a call to become home missionaries to a tribe of American Indians on a reservation in Arizona. This decision set the course for the rest of their married lives; their missionary service was followed eventually by full-time service in the pastoral ministry, often depending on the uneven financial support of their congregations. Jim is presently serving, however, as the salaried senior pastor of a large church in California.

Last summer Jim and Mary's four children planned an elaborate reaffirmation ceremony for their parents' 40th wedding anniversary and my husband and I were invited to attend. Other than the 25th anniversary ceremony of Barbara Mandrell and her husband, which I had watched on television, I had never seen a full-fledged reaffirmation wedding ceremony with all the trimmings. Jim and Mary's service was held in the elegantly decorated sanctuary of the church they pastored and Mary was given away by her older brother. Their children served as their attendants, their grandsons as ushers and their young granddaughters as bell ringers (girls who travel up and down the aisles ringing delicate crystal bells to announce the beginning of the ceremony).

Their children, who are gifted singers and musicians, provided the music and their eldest daughter made a professional-looking three-tiered wedding cake, complete with Jim and Mary's original bride-and-groom cake topper that had been carefully packed away for 40 years.

The minister who had married them in 1955 came out of retirement to conduct the service and wrote these personalized vows that reflected the couple's life of sacrificial service to God and to each other:

Minister: "When I married you on that August afternoon in 1955, you had no idea what God had in store for you: your service as missionaries under very difficult circumstances, often doing without the necessities of life as you depended on the love offerings of others for your survival. When you took your wedding vows that day you promised to love each other whether 'richer or poorer,' and you kept that vow as you remained true to each other and true to your Lord through those difficult times. Your circumstances required great faith, and your faith never wavered. I know you count all your hardships as sheer joy, however, because of the blessings He has given you: four children who love and respect you; nine adoring grandchildren; and much fruit in your ministry.

*And so, as you come today to reaffirm your wedding
vows and as you reflect back over all your years
together as husband and wife, do you now reaffirm
the vows you took 40 years ago? If so, repeat them
after me:*

*'I, _____, take you, _____, to be my
husband / wife; to have and to hold from this day
forward, for better, for worse, for richer, for poorer, in
sickness and in health, to love and to cherish always.' "*

After their vows were affirmed and it was time for Jim to
kiss his bride, he surprised everyone, including her, by pre-
senting her with a diamond suspended on a delicate gold
chain. What had everyone in tears—at least, all the women
present—was the look of love in Jim's eyes as he fastened
the gold chain around Mary's neck and murmured some
very quiet and private words of endearment before he
kissed her. It was obvious to all that they are still very
much in love.

*"On _____ 19 ____, we took our vows
as we stood in this very place. My knees were shaking
as I recall, and although I gave my heart to you that
day as I recited my vows, I spoke haltingly, feeling
some apprehension as we entered the fearful state of
matrimony. As I look back now, surveying our years
of married life, I have a grateful reminiscence in my
heart because of the blessed fulfillment our marriage
has been. I give thanks to God for our life together
which has been rich beyond measure, and today I
reaffirm my wedding vows, but this time with a
clearer head and absolute assurance in my heart.
There are no hesitations or second thoughts today as I
promise with all my heart to love and cherish you for*

all the blessed days God may yet allow us to live together on this earth."

♥ ♥ ♥ ♥

"You are still my bride, my precious one, as beautiful and lovely as the day I married you on _____, 19___. You are the most important person in my life and I intend to keep it that way. Our marriage has succeeded, while so many have failed, because we have kept the laughter and thrown out the pain; although we have winked at life and laughed at its transient problems, we have always taken our marriage seriously. Yes, marriage is a fragile thing, and one that has lasted as long as ours is a precious rarity, to be held carefully and cherished forever. As we celebrate our _____ anniversary today, in the presence of these witnesses, I hereby reaffirm my vows, spoken first on that day in 19___, to love you, comfort you, honor and keep you in sickness and in health, in sorrow and in joy, and to be faithful to you as long as we both shall live."

♥ ♥ ♥ ♥

"My dear _____, you are a revered wife / husband and mother / father, always filling our hearts with your love. You have kept our home peaceful and have been a gracious host / hostess to all who have graced us through the years. Your children rise up and call you blessed, and your friends stand by you, eternally grateful for the love you have extended as you've helped and comforted those in need. You are the most unselfish man / woman I know and I consider it an honor to have been married to you for _____ years. Today, in the presence of God and this

precious company of friends and family, I freely and publicly renew my wedding vows, pledging again my unwavering love as your faithful husband/wife from this day forward. May the Lord bless us with many more happy years together."

"I can't believe how lucky I was to find you _____ years ago, and I was luckier still when you agreed to marry me. And hasn't our marriage been good, with so many memories of beautiful moments shared? I treasure those memories...they are souvenirs in my heart... memories of you as my friend, my lover, my husband/ wife. Our marriage is the most important thing in my life, and you are the most important person. As our love has grown deeper each year and more comfortable, too, our relationship has gone beyond anything I could have imagined and as we stand before this gathering of our friends and family, I publicly and joyfully reaffirm our wedding vows."

"_____ years ago, I chose you to be my husband/ wife, and today I choose you again, not because I should, not because it is expected, not because I have no other choice, but because my love for you is even richer and deeper than the day I married you, and I choose you again gladly and without reservation. Choosing each other is an ongoing process, my love, and every morning, as I look at your precious face, I choose you anew and rejoice in the fact that you have chosen me, too. How blessed I am to have you as my husband/wife. You have met all my expectations and given me a life filled with joy. I want to live with you

"Thank you, _____, for being such a kind, nurturing, loving husband / wife and father / mother. I am so grateful to have found you at such a young age, and that our friendship grew into a love that committed itself to a lifelong marriage. After _____ years of living with you, loving you, and appreciating you, my love for you has deepened and matured, and today, as we stand before our family to reaffirm our wedding vows, I do so with a heart that is overflowing with my love for you, my cherished husband / wife. I give you every measure of myself, committing myself to you anew, as we look forward to the wonderful, challenging years yet in store for us as a married couple."

♥ ♥ ♥ ♥

Woman to her husband: "When I was a young woman, I had dreams of being married someday, and when you came along, you were truly my Knight in Shining Armor. After _____ years of marriage, I can honestly say, as God is my witness, that you have been all I could have imagined or hoped for: my lover, my companion, my friend, my nurturer, my comforter, my playmate, and a model father. I am so lucky to have found you and I pray to be worthy of such a man; today, as we celebrate our anniversary, I gladly and joyfully take you again as my husband and I promise anew, as I vowed on our wedding day, to love and respect you, for richer or poorer, in sickness or in health, for better or worse, until death do us part. Thank you for being my Knight in Shining Armor."

♥ ♥ ♥ ♥

for the rest of my life, not because I should, or because it is expected, but because that is the longing of my heart."

♥ ♥ ♥ ♥

"I fell in love with you the first time when we were in high school, remember? And throughout our married life, I have fallen in love with you again hundreds of times for a hundred different reasons. We've shared our dreams and built our castles in the air, but when things have been rough and I've been afraid, yours is the hand I want to hold—you are the source of my strength. You are still the only man / woman for me and when I think of the years that still lie ahead of us, I fall totally and completely in love with you all over again. How I love you at this moment, _____, and I vow to be a good and faithful husband / wife for all the rest of our days."

♥ ♥ ♥ ♥

Man to his wife: "I remember that Saturday morning, ____ years ago, when you walked down the aisle and into my arms, my beautiful bride. We had such great expectations of each other, didn't we? We hoped that every day would be as glorious and happy as that day. Every day wasn't as glorious and happy as that day, as we discovered through our years together, but you never disappointed me; your love was constant and steady; you were always there for me, no matter what the circumstances. How I love you still, my beautiful bride, and how proud I am to be your husband. I gladly renew the promises I made to you ____ years ago, and I pledge myself to you again this day with a love as fresh as the day I married you."

♥ ♥ ♥ ♥

"You are mine, my love, and I am yours, as ordained by God from the beginning of time. He brought us together and He has kept us together, to love and be loved, to cherish and be cherished for all the days of our lives. You are God's gift to me, my priceless treasure, my blessing for life. May He bless us as we come together today to renew our pledge of love to one another."

♥ ♥ ♥ ♥

"Remember the first time we met? You were dancing with someone else; I cut in on that poor soul, and we have been dancing together ever since. Our life's dance has been a steady dance, weaving in and out of our days and years together, a quiet, intimate dance of shared thoughts and dreams, through many summers of new-mown grass, through cold, chilling winters, through seasons of tears and laughter. Today we continue our life's dance with a commitment that is as fresh and joyous as the day I married you. Dance with me, _____, until the day I die."

(Personalize this vow to reflect your own meeting and life together.)

♥ ♥ ♥ ♥

"Do you remember all our years together, _____? There have been _____ of them. There were those first years, when we were so excited about being married and having our babies. Then, there were those difficult years as we struggled to raise teenagers in a dangerous world. Finally, there were

the empty-nest years when our children married and went out on their own. But as I reflect back on all our married days, and I picture you the times you sat feeding _____ in the big rocker in the den, and that Halloween you dressed up like Big Bird for _____'s party, and the time in the hospital when you held me close after my accident...all these remembrances fill my heart to overflowing with my love for you. You have been a devoted, loving wife / husband and mother / father and there are no words to express how deep and rich is the love I feel for you this day. I am proud to be your husband / wife and I gladly renew my vows as we celebrate our _____ anniversary."

(Insert your own personal memories into these vows.)

♥ ♥ ♥ ♥

" _____, you have been my all, m[...] for all these years, a loving devoted mother / fat[...] and grandmother / grandfather, always giving [...] yourself with Christ-like, sacrificial love. You [...] our needs and cares above your own, always [...] nourishing and supporting—a Godly man / [...] seeking His help in all ways and living His [...] through your words and deeds. I come to y[...] my precious, adored husband / wife and g[...] you afresh and anew, as we renew our w[...] first pledged _____ years ago, in [...] In the presence of our family and frien[...] today and I vow to be a faithful husb[...] this day forward, for as long as the L[...] on this earth."

♥ ♥ ♥ ♥

"_____, thank you for your love and your faithfulness to me all these years. It's easy to love someone at first, when we look our best, say the right thing, and are always on our best behavior; but you have seen me at my absolute worst, and still you love me, which makes me love you all the more. Thank you for always being there for me, in every way, and thank you for all you will be to me in the years to come. I pledge again to you this day to love you for the rest of our days."

"Twenty-five years ago today we took our wedding vows, and though many things have changed in our lives since then, one thing has remained constant: our love. We had babies and watched them grow up; we built three homes and sold them; we've moved 12 times; we've owned 17 cars; we've suffered through times of illness and times when the paycheck didn't stretch to pay the bills. But through it all, my love for you has remained; in fact, although it seems impossible, I believe I love you more every year we are married. I'm so glad I married you that day 25 years ago, and I gladly renew my wedding vows this day. I promise to love you, honor you, cherish and keep you, for better or worse, for richer or poorer, for all the years of our lives. _____, I want you to know that whatever may face us in the years to come, I will always love you."

(Personalize this to reflect your own life together.)

"_____, what a good marriage we have had for 25 years! Who would ever believe that after all these years we love each other even more than we did on our wedding day? In fact, our love has been a precious love—so beautiful and rare. You have been everything a wife / husband could ever hope for: a compassionate friend; a caring listener; a patient nurse; an exemplary mother / father; and an enthusiastic partner as we have pursued our dreams and goals. Thank you for making me so happy in every way; you are still my sweetheart and I gladly reaffirm my wedding vows this day."_

"_Fifty years...50 golden years! How I praise God for you, _____. It was such a stroke of luck to have met you that day at the Canteen, and yet, was it really luck, or God's providence? I loved you from that first time I saw you as you stood there with those glorious auburn curls and those sparkling emerald eyes. Who would have believed you would ever give me a chance? But, you did...and now, over 50 years later, I still love you as much as I did that first time I saw you. When we married we promised to be faithful in good times and in bad, whether richer or poorer, in sickness and in health, and we have had our share of all of these, haven't we? But we have been faithful and our love has grown as we have overcome many obstacles over our 50 years of marriage. How can I thank you for the joy you have brought into my life, for your laughter, your hugs and your constant, unshakable love? I recommit myself to you this day, _____, as your husband / wife, and I_

promise to love you always, just as I did 50 years ago, and just as I do today."

(Personalize these vows to include the way you met, the color of hair and eyes, etc.)

♥ ♥ ♥ ♥

Up close and personal

This chapter wouldn't be complete without the story of a golden anniversary couple.

Erma Streeter and Loren Hosmer knew each other all their lives, but fell in love when they were teenagers in the 1940s. They realized their love had turned to marriage-type love, however, during the summer of 1945 when she was 17 and he was 20. It all began one Saturday in June when Erma and her sister, Fern, walked from their home to the Uptown Ballroom at 10th and G streets in Modesto, California where Loren asked Erma to dance. A week and a half later Loren showed up at Erma's home unannounced and asked her out on a date, "right in front of all of my family," as Erma writes. He took her to a carnival where he conveniently steered her over to the Fun House where her pleated skirt just happened to blow over her head as a gust of air suddenly spurted from beneath the floor boards. Embarrassed, Erma turned to Loren and asked, "Did you see anything?" With a smirk, he said no, but years later he told her it was "just a good thing you were wearing panties."

They dated nearly every day after that and he proposed a few months later when he told her he loved her and wanted her to be the mother of his children. (He didn't tell her there would be *eight* of them!)

Their parents weren't keen on them getting married, so Erma and Loren decided to elope. On December 30, 1945 they took off for Carson City, Nevada, where they were married in a Presbyterian parsonage. The minister's wife, daughter and grandson were their witnesses. They only had a one-night honeymoon in Reno before returning to their respective homes where they kept their marriage a secret. When their parents found out about the wedding a month later, they "weren't all that happy" but, finally, three months after the wedding, Erma's family had a shower for them where they passed out wedding announcements to the guests in attendance.

Throughout their 50 years of married life they struggled along, raising eight children, their times very difficult at first as they lived with rationed tires, gasoline, sugar, meat and shoes, something many of you reading this chapter know all about. Loren held many positions through the years: school bus driver, carpenter, contractor and, most recently, as owner of the Capital Door Sales Company. Erma worked for the National Can Company, as well as the Census Bureau; she also helped in the family business as secretary and bookkeeper.

They lost one of their children, their dear daughter, Nancy Lea Smith, when she died in a single automobile accident in 1984, but their remaining seven children, plus their 21 grandchildren, seven great-grandchildren and other family members and friends honored them with a lovely 50th wedding anniversary celebration on December 30, 1995. There were 200 guests present to witness the reaffirmation of their vows. Five of their daughters and one granddaughter served as bridesmaids; two sons and two grandsons as groomsmen and the rest of their grandchildren, great-grandchildren and other family members served in many ways, as well—as flower girls, musicians, vocalists, readers, guest book attendant, "balloon engineers," disc jockey, and the myriad duties required to pull off such a glorious occasion. Loren and Erma have graciously allowed me to share the vow segment of their reaffirmation service with you.

Norma and Larry (Erma's sister and brother-in-law) delivered this reading that preceded their vows:

> *"The home is to provide the sweetest, most precious and endearing relationship on earth. The value can best be described by the words, 'Sweeter as the years go by.' Marriage is a lifelong contract. It is not entered into thoughtlessly or lightly. Loren and Erma have realized that mind, heart and soul have become one and they wish to renew their wedding vows to bind them the rest of their days. God has blessed this union as His word has been reverenced, loved and relied on. Obedience to Him is the prime of their responsibilities. Consequently, they wish to create a bond of lasting love and devotion to each other for the rest of their days."*
>
> *Minister: "Please join hands and repeat after me:"*
>
> *Loren (repeating after the minister): "I, Loren, promise to continue to love and cherish and protect Erma, whose hand I now hold, and provide for her in health and sickness, and be true to her, and cleave to her until death do us part. I renew my vow to take her for my lawful wedded wife."*
>
> *Erma (repeating after the minister): "I, Erma, promise to continue to love and honor this man, Loren, whose hand I now hold, and be true and faithful to him and cleave to him until death do us part. I renew my vow to take him for my lawful wedded husband."*

Minister: "I do by the virtue of authority vested in me as a minister of the gospel and the authority of the Father, sanction your desire to reaffirm your wedding vows."

I wish I could include a photograph of Loren and Erma! If you could only see them, you would agree with me that they absolutely radiate with joy. Oh, that we could all look that good and be that happy after 50 years of married life!

♥ ♥ ♥ ♥

"_____, I'm glad I had the good sense to marry you 50 years ago. They've been good years as we survived everything the world had to throw at us: those Depression years, when we made our own soap and ate by candlelight every night because we couldn't afford electricity; juggling two jobs at once when the children were growing up; those painful times of separation when I served in the Navy during the war; the day we lost our stock in the range fire; and your surgery two years ago. We've been through a lot together, but our love has survived it all and we deserve to celebrate. I love you, my darling husband / wife, as much today as the day I married you and I'm happy to commit myself to you as your loving husband / wife for at least 50 more years!"

(Personalize these vows with your own memories.)

♥ ♥ ♥ ♥

"When we were married _____ years ago today, I thought I knew what love was. I was in love with you, that I knew for sure; but, as I look back on all our years together, I realize now that our love at its beginning, although it was real and sure, was only a

shallow imitation of the love I feel for you today. Every year, in your dear, precious way, you have made me love you more and more. And why? Because the more I know you, the more I love you. You are worthy of a deep, holy love, and that is what I feel for you today as I gladly recommit my heart and life to you."

"On this day _____ years ago, I promised to love you and cherish you all the days of my life. I hereby reaffirm that promise, in the presence of God and our family. _____, you have been my friend and companion and the revered mother / father of our children, but, most of all, you have been my beautiful loving bride / handsome loving husband for all these years, and I renew my pledge to you today of my eternal devotion."

Reaffirmation vows with the wine ceremony

(The couple sips from the same glass or silver cup and then recites these vows.)

"As we drink together from this cup of wine, so may we continue in a perfect union of love and devotion to each other as we continue to draw contentment, comfort and felicity from the cup of life, and thereby find life's joys doubly gladdening and its bitterness sweetened by our true companionship and love."

♥ ♥ ♥ ♥

If you are having a formal reaffirmation ceremony or if you enjoy the classics, look in Chapter 9 for the reaffirmation selections, including writings by Shakespeare, Kahlil Gibran, John Keats, Robert and Elizabeth Browning, Walt Whitman and Anne Bradstreet.

Chapter 6

Vows for Older Couples

Personalized wedding vows carry special significance when a man or woman finds "the one" much later in life, after many years of searching, or when a man or woman loses a long-time mate to death or divorce, then finds another and marries again. Here are several choices contributed by older brides and grooms.

"_____, *we have suffered much in this life, each in our own way, and what a miracle it is to find each other now, just when we need each other the most. I want to take care of you now, to be your shelter and your light, putting the past behind us as we face a joyous new life together for our remaining years. How I thank God for sending you*

to me, to stand beside me, to hold me and to share your life with me. I need you and I love you more than words can say, and I pledge to you now, with this holy vow, to be your true and faithful husband / wife from this day forward and forevermore."

"We have experienced the joys and sorrows of life through our many years on this earth. We have loved and married before and raised our families in the fear of the Lord. And then, in our twilight years, when we least expected it, God, in His divine providence, has brought us together with a love and a joy as fresh as our youth. How I thank God for bringing you to me, my friend, my companion, my precious jewel. I hereby pledge myself to be your faithful husband / wife with a love that will endure for all the rest of our days."

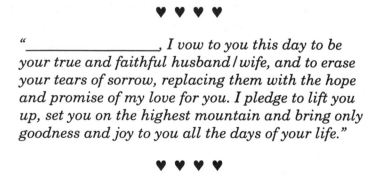

"_____, I vow to you this day to be your true and faithful husband / wife, and to erase your tears of sorrow, replacing them with the hope and promise of my love for you. I pledge to lift you up, set you on the highest mountain and bring only goodness and joy to you all the days of your life."

"_____, until you came into my life, my heart was hollow; but your love has filled my heart and made me whole. We have both shed tears of loneliness after the loss of our mates, but our love has chased those shadows away and brought gladness

and rejoicing to our frightened souls. I pledge to you now my love for all time as I ask you to become my husband / wife. From this day forward I promise to love you with all my heart, withholding nothing."

"In the presence of God, our children and grandchildren, I take you, _____, to be my wedded husband / wife. I promise to love you, honor you and cherish you, in sickness and in health, in good times and in bad, so long as we both shall live. May the Lord bless us with many happy years together and may the peace of Christ live always in our hearts and in our home as we become one."

"Because of you, I'm no longer lonely; because of you, my life is brand new; because of you, my heart is singing—no more sorrows, no more tears. Because of you, my days are filled with hope and excitement, just to be with you, letting your love soak into my dry bones until they are strong and filled with your energy. I am young again, dear _____, all because of you. I need you now and always, every waking moment, and I freely and wholly give myself to you this day, to be your loving and faithful husband / wife, and to be true to you always, as long as the Lord gives us together in this life."

"_____, we are God's children, not young in years, but infinitely young at heart, as we join together, in the presence of our family and

friends, as man and wife. We both have assurance
that it was God's will that we met and fell in love,
and so it is with a grateful heart, that I,
_____, take you, _____, this
day as my husband/wife, that we may live together
as partners for eternity. May we always seek God
first in our marriage and thank Him daily for
giving us the gift of each other."

♥ ♥ ♥ ♥

"_____, you have brought light into the
darkness of my life, music to my quiet days and
laughter to my solemn nights. You have revived me
and given wings to my heart; keepsake my heart
within your soul and, just as the hawk flies high
overhead on the wings of the wind, so I will soar on
the promise of your love. I give you, from this day
forward, the gift of myself, my love and all that I am.
I will fill up the wounds in your heart, just as you will
fill mine. In good times or in bad, I will stand by your
side and I will die with my love for you still
untarnished in my heart."

♥ ♥ ♥ ♥

"_____, I choose you to be my wife/
husband. You are the one I adore; you are the one I
cherish; you are the one I honor. At this late time of
my life, you have startled me out of a deep sleep with
your unexpectedly beautiful love. I receive you into the
very breath of my soul, to be the light of my life, to fill
my glad heart with a joy beyond all imaginings. I will
hold your heart tenderly in the palms of my hands,

*cherishing it, thanking God for it. I give myself to
you this day and I promise to be faithful to you for as
long as we both shall live."*

*"I take you this day as my wife / husband because you
are my beloved, the one I have chosen to journey with
me through my remaining days. You are my princess /
prince, my companion, my lover and my friend, and I
promise that wherever our journey leads and whatever
its outcome, I will love you, cherish you and be
faithful to you, as God is my witness."*

*"You have brought me back from the dead, my sweet
one. Just when everything seemed dark and hopeless,
God sent you to me, my bright ray of life. Your beauty
surrounds you and the world is a better place because
of your loving heart. It is beyond comprehension that I
should be so blessed to be loved by you. You have
made life worth living again and I thank God we will
spend it together, sharing our constant love and
devotion, soul mates, together at last. I hereby vow,
humbly before God, in the presence of our friends and
family, to be your faithful husband / wife in whatever
circumstances life may bring us through all the years
He allows us to live."*

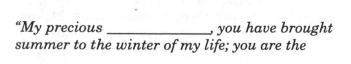

*"My precious _____, you have brought
summer to the winter of my life; you are the*

sunshine after the storm, my glorious hope of a new day. What have I done to deserve such good fortune, such a prize as you? I haven't the words to express the joy you have brought into my life and I wholly and unreservedly take you as my wife/husband on this, our wedding day. I promise to love you, honor you, cherish and respect you always, until death do us part."

"_____, I take you as my life's partner in marriage for all the days God shall yet give us to live on this earth. I promise to love you, honor you, praise you, serve you, listen to you, encourage you and stand by you always, even in times of illness and crisis. I promise to laugh with you when you laugh, cry with you with you cry and hold you fast beside me until the gates of death finally open and separate us."

♥ ♥ ♥ ♥

Up close and personal

I would like to tell you about a couple who were married three years ago; they were ages 76 and 73 at the time. I'm not going to tell you who they are because I don't want to embarrass them, so I'll call them Horace and Emma. Horace and Emma were married to their first-loves for more than 50 years and both of them, also, were caregivers to their mates up until their mates passed away. Meanwhile, throughout all their years of married life, the two couples became quite close, traveling together, square dancing together and truly loving each other as dear friends.

When each lost their mate, it was only natural for them to spend time together, consoling each other and trying to bear each other up under such a devastating loss. Well, one thing led to another, and within six months or so, people noticed them holding hands and snuggling in public, so it wasn't surprising when they decided to get married. I attended their wedding and these were their eloquently written vows:

> *Horace: "Emma, we have lived long, full lives and experienced many joys and sorrows. We have each raised our families in the fear and admonition of the Lord, releasing them finally to their own joys and sorrows to be found in this world. Then, when we lost our loving mates and our hearts were full of pain, God brought us to each other so that we may find joy again. And what a joy you are to me, my precious Emma, my dear one, God's gift to me. I'm so thankful for you and I give myself to you this day, freely and without reservation, as I vow to be your loving, faithful husband for all the days we have left together on this earth."*

> *Emma: "We have lived long lives, and we wouldn't trade our lives for any prize the world could offer, but, because of you, life is more precious to me today than it has ever been before. You have brought me a joy and fresh anticipation of a happy new life yet to come as I take you as my husband. As we stand here before our friends and family, our children and grandchildren, I publicly declare my love for you. I want them to know how proud I am of you and how special is our love. I give myself to*

*you, Horace, on this our wedding day, and I
promise to be your faithful wife for all the years
that God may give us together on this earth."*

Soon after they married they moved to Missouri to be
closer to his children, but they were back in California recently to attend the funeral of one of their close friends and
I overheard Horace—now 79 years old, mind you—as he
confided to one of his old buddies at the reception that
followed: "I'm telling you, Harry, she's an awful lot of fun
when the sun goes down, if you know what I mean."

I glanced at Emma to see if she may have overheard his
remark; she had and was blushing like a newlywed bride
on the morning after.

At *any* age...ain't love grand?

Chapter 7

Vows With Religious Variations

Many couples want their vows to have deep spiritual meaning, reflecting their personal faith in God, as well as their religious heritage. This chapter includes many of these vows, with hundreds of phrasings from which to choose. Most are based on scripture, prayer or the religious commitment of the bride and groom, not only to each other but to their God as well.

♥ ♥ ♥ ♥

"I take you, _____, as my lawfully wedded wife / husband according to God's holy ordinance. I feel blessed beyond words and favored beyond measure that God brought you into my life. I promise to be faithful to you, giving you honor, respect and understanding as we strive to live in harmony and humility, in times of great or plenty, sickness or health, knowing that our marriage has been sanctioned by God and that our lives are fully entrusted to Him."

♥ ♥ ♥ ♥

"_____, you are my beloved bride / bridegroom whom I choose to marry this day. I know that marriage is a holy union, instituted by God in the Garden of Eden when He saw that it was not good for man to live alone. Marriage was also given a crown of glory by the Apostle Paul, who likened it to that Holy union which exists between Christ and His church. Because of the deep, holy spiritual significance of marriage, I therefore enter it reverently, knowing that the Lord will richly bless those who seek His favour. I come into this holy relationship this day to be joined with you, _____, as your lawfully wedded husband / wife and I pray that our hearts will be melded together by the holy seal of God's approval as we become one flesh."

♥ ♥ ♥ ♥

"_____, I promise to be your faithful husband / wife, loving you and serving you with all my heart, just as my heart also longs to love and serve God. I enter into this holy estate of matrimony with great reverence, soberly and discreetly, in the fear of

God, realizing that marriage is instituted by Him, signifying the mystical union that is between Christ and His church. And just as Christ gave Himself for His church, so I give myself unreservedly to you on this, our wedding day."

♥ ♥ ♥ ♥

"_____, I commit my love to you this day for as long as we both shall live; this love is the very flame of God and may no man dare to quench it. I promise to be faithful to you, to nurture you, to cherish you and encourage you, with the same care and concern that I give myself. I promise to help you become all the woman / man our Lord has intended you to be, and throughout our lifetime together, you will always be my beloved wife / husband and my best friend."

♥ ♥ ♥ ♥

"It is the deepest desire of my heart and the holy will of God Almighty that I give myself to you as your husband / wife, to walk with you in riches or poverty, in sickness or in health, in good times or bad. I will always stand by your side, praying for you, supporting you and encouraging you and I will always seek to communicate with you, never holding anything back, so that we may be one unified spirit, until death do us part."

♥ ♥ ♥ ♥

"_____, I come to you this day in holy reverence as I take you as my husband / wife. I thank God that He, in His holy providence, has given us to

*each other. My prayer is that our hearts will be
melded together this day with God's seal of approval
and that I will be a good and faithful husband/wife,
always providing you with emotional and spiritual
nourishment, supporting you in every way. May we
live together in such a way that it will be evident to all
that we have a deep, abiding love for each other and
for our God and Heavenly Father. May God bless our
marriage for all the days of our lives."*

♥ ♥ ♥ ♥

*Groom (to his bride): "_____, God, our
Father, is the One Who established marriage; it was
His plan, and therefore it is only with His help and
blessing that we dare take this great step in our lives.
My prayer is that I will be a husband worthy of your
praise, your faithful provider and protector, and your
haven from harm. I promise to be tender,
understanding and true to you always, for all the days
God may give us on this earth."*

*Bride (to her groom): "_____, I have an
abiding faith in God, and I, too, take this great step of
marriage with reverence. I promise to hold fast to my
faith in Him and in you, as my dear husband. I
realize that marriage is not merely the act of living
together and pleasing each other, but of living for God
and pleasing Him, and I pray that He will give us a
great spiritual purpose in our life together."*

♥ ♥ ♥ ♥

*"_____, it is with unspeakable joy that I
take you to be my wedded wife/husband, that
together we may become one. As Christ loves His*

Body, the Church, so I promise to love you with an
unselfish devotion. I will care for you with tenderness
and I will always seek to strengthen you, comfort you,
encourage you and hold you up daily in prayer before
our Heavenly Father. I pledge you my faithfulness
and eternal love from this day forward."

♥ ♥ ♥ ♥

Bride: "I, _____, take you, _____,
as my husband."

Groom: "I, _____, take you, _____,
as my wife."

Bride: "I promise to be a faithful wife."

Groom: "I promise to be a faithful husband."

Bride: "May our life together be a sign of Christ's love
to a broken world."

Groom: "May our deep, abiding love for each other be
a sign of our everlasting bond."

Bride: "May we each be a strength to the other."

Groom: "And may we seek to comfort in sorrow and be
companions in joy."

Bride: "May we be willing to accept our faults..."

Groom: "And to seek each other's forgiveness."

Bride: "May God bless our marriage covenant."

Groom: "And may our lives be lived in the fullness of
His love, for now and forevermore."

Bride: "For now and forevermore."

♥ ♥ ♥ ♥

Up close and personal

When Warren and Verna Riopel told me how they met and fell in love, I decided their story was as poignant and as "goose-pimply" as any romantic movie script ever written, from *Shadowlands* to *Sleepless in Seattle*. You see, Verna was a 33-year-old schoolteacher who owned her own home and 19 acres of productive grapevines. Her life was full and satisfying, except for one thing: She was still looking for "Mr. Right"—the man whom God had chosen as her life's companion.

Along came Warren, a man in his mid-30s, the "new guy in town" who planned to enroll at the local university in the fall. Warren met Verna one Sunday at church and it soon became known that he, being the typically destitute American college student, needed a job if he was to survive the summer and have enough money to enroll for the fall semester.

The summer work season was just beginning at Verna's vineyard and, *of course*, it was perfectly understandable that she needed help with the annual weeding, so Warren offered to help her pull the weeds if she would promise to cook him just one home-cooked meal per day. As Warren labored shoulder-to-shoulder with Verna under the hot California Central Valley sun, it was only natural that he worked up quite a thirst, so, *of course*, it was only logical for Verna to join him for an icy cold lemonade. And, *of course*, a man can't work straight through without a little rest in the shade every so often, so, *of course*, it was only logical for Verna to join him occasionally—after all, it wasn't polite to leave a guy sitting there all alone.

Well...after a few dozen jugs of lemonade, many hours visiting under the shade of the big oak tree, and plate after plate of good home cooking, they realized, *of course*, that they had fallen in love and were meant to be and by that September they were engaged to be married. They knew in their hearts that God had brought them together that summer and their personalized wedding vows reflected this assurance:

> *Minister: "Will you, Warren Riopel, have Verna Plett to be your wedded wife, and do you solemnly promise that you will loyally fulfill your obligations as her husband, to protect her, to honor her, and to cherish her in adversity as well as in prosperity, and to keep yourself unto her alone so long as you both shall live?"*
>
> *Warren: "I will."*
>
> *Minister: "Will you, Verna Plett, have Warren Riopel to be your wedded husband, and do you solemnly promise that you will be unto him a tender, loving and true wife, in sunshine and shadow alike, and to be faithful to him so long as you both shall live?"*
>
> *Verna: "I will."*
>
> *Warren (to Verna) and Verna (to Warren):*
> *"_____, I acknowledge God's presence in our lives and I believe that He has led us together to share our lives with each other, so I pledge to you my undying love, my respect, my devotion, and my life, without reservation from this moment on. I promise that, with God's help, I will be a faithful, loving wife/husband, and that whether times are easy or hard, I will always remember that each of us is meant for the other, with Christ as the head of our home."*

By the way, Verna still teaches school and they live in her home on the 19 acres where Warren is now a full-time dairy farmer. She's still feeding him pretty good, and if you should happen to drive out their country road some warm summer afternoon, you'll probably find them sharing a lemonade under the shade of that same old oak tree.

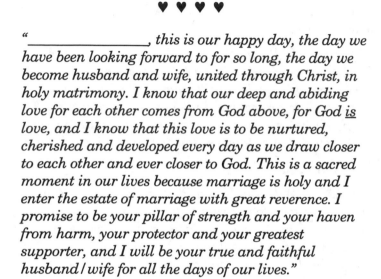

"_____, this is our happy day, the day we have been looking forward to for so long, the day we become husband and wife, united through Christ, in holy matrimony. I know that our deep and abiding love for each other comes from God above, for God *is* love, and I know that this love is to be nurtured, cherished and developed every day as we draw closer to each other and ever closer to God. This is a sacred moment in our lives because marriage is holy and I enter the estate of marriage with great reverence. I promise to be your pillar of strength and your haven from harm, your protector and your greatest supporter, and I will be your true and faithful husband / wife for all the days of our lives."

♥ ♥ ♥ ♥

"I promise to be a faithful husband / wife, to care for you in loving devotion, to be your strength when you are in need, to be your counselor in your perplexity, to be your comfort in sorrow, to be your companion in joy. I promise to pray for you, uphold you and defend you and to seek your forgiveness if I should ever hurt you in any way. I make this vow before God and these witnesses."

♥ ♥ ♥ ♥

"_____, you are God's perfect gift to me, an unspeakable blessing to my life. In my wildest dreams I could have never imagined someone as dear

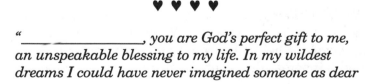

and precious as you, someone I could love so deeply and with such total devotion. Just as God gave Eve to Adam as his helpmate, so that he would be complete, so God has given you to me. I vow to try, with God's help, to be everything He wants me to be for you: your comforter, your helper, your encourager, your provider and your servant. As we begin our life together today as husband and wife, I gladly lay down all my rights, so that I can be to you everything you need. May God bless our marriage and make us pleasing to Him."

"_____, I take you as my lawfully wedded husband / wife and I hereby pledge myself to be faithful, an example of Christ's love in our home, that our lives together as a married couple may be a sign of His love and concern for the world. I give myself wholly to you this hour and I promise to guard, cherish and protect you all the days of my life."

"I, _____, take you, _____, as my cherished wedded husband. It is the greatest desire of my heart to be faithful to you and to love you always, seeking to meet your every need, desiring to help you in every way, listening to you, encouraging you, comforting you and standing by your side in whatever circumstances may face us in the years ahead. I will respect you, honor you and strive for harmony in our marriage with a quiet and gentle spirit. As God created Eve for Adam, so I shall be a helper to you always, from this day forth and for as long as we both shall live."

♥ ♥ ♥ ♥

"_____, because of our faith in God and our assurance that He has brought us together, I come to this ceremony in reverence and awe. I vow to be a faithful husband / wife to you. I promise to put God first in our marriage, depending on him for guidance and wisdom as we seek His will in our married life. I realize that marriage, like our creation as man and woman, owes its very existence to God, and so I take this commitment seriously. I come into this holy union without reservation and I give myself to you for companionship, help and comfort, in prosperity or in adversity, for all the days of our lives."

♥ ♥ ♥ ♥

"_____, as marriage has been established by God, I willingly bind myself to you this day in love, even as Christ is One with the Church, His body. Just as nothing can separate us from the love of God in Christ, nothing can separate us as husband and wife, as I pledge the same steadfast love to you. I promise, with God's help, to be your faithful husband / wife, to love and serve you as Christ commands, as long as we both shall live."

♥ ♥ ♥ ♥

"_____, because God has given you to me as my own, I also give myself to you this day. I promise to be a patient and tolerant husband / wife, to forgive freely, as our Lord has forgiven us, and, above everything else, to be truly loving, faithful, and always thankful. My love for you will outlast everything; it

*will stand when all else has fallen. I promise this as a
solemn vow before God and man."*

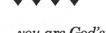

"_____, *you are God's priceless gift to
me. You are my beloved, my friend, my dove, my
perfect one. Your voice is sweet. Put me like a seal over
your heart. I take you as my wife / husband from this
day forward, to join with you and share our lives
together and be true to you with my whole being. My
commitment is made in love, to be kept in faith, lived
in hope and eternally made new."*

(Based on verses in the Song of Solomon in the Bible.)

*"We are here today because of a miracle, the miracle of
our love. I come to you with a pure heart as I commit
myself to you as your husband / wife; I promise to
walk with you from this day forward as your life
partner, always searching for God's will in our lives,
and trusting Him for His blessings. He may bless our
union with children, and if we are so blessed, we will
praise Him for yet another miracle of love in our
lives."*

"_____, *I believe that marriage is
ordained by God, and so, today I marry you in the
spirit of Christian joy to become united with you as
one. Our lives have been touched by His love, a love as
soft as the dawn, as radiant as the sun, as bright as
the moon and as beautiful as the rainbow that enfolds
us after a storm. I give you my heart this day; open*

*your heart and lock mine inside. I give you my life;
open yours and let me become one with you. Just as
the flower opens to the warmth of the sun, so shall our
marriage blossom as it basks in the warmth of our
love. May this love be always bright, always beautiful
and always new; this is the first day of our life
together."*

*Minister: "Do you, _____, promise your
Heavenly Father to take _____, to be
your wife / husband, to love and care for her / him, in
the good that may light your way, and in the
misfortunes that may darken your day, and to be true
to her / him in all circumstances until death alone
shall part you?"*

Bride / Groom: "I do."

*Bride: "The ever-blessed God Almighty has brought us
together by His providence."*

*Groom: "He has enriched us with His grace and
sanctified us by His Spirit."*

*Bride: "Today is the day our lives will be changed
forever."*

*Groom: "From this day forward, we will cherish each
other as husband and wife."*

*Bride: "We will hold each other with mutual esteem
and love."*

*Groom: "We will bear with each other's infirmities
and weaknesses."*

Bride: "We will comfort each other in sickness, trouble and sorrow."

Groom: "We will pray for each other and encourage each other."

Bride: "We will surprise each other with the joy, wonder and miracle of marriage."

Groom: "We will be warm to each other with affection and laughter."

Bride: "Our love will bear all things and believe all things."

Groom: "Our love will hope all things and endure all things."

Bride: "Our love will outlast everything."

Groom: "We will love each other forever, just as we love each other this day."

Bride: "Yes...just as we do this day."

"Before God brought you into my life, I walked alone; now I have you at my side and we walk together. You are my strength and my priceless treasure. I cherish you, adore you and thank God for you. Just as the Bible says that God dwells in us and his love is perfected in us, so God knew us both and chose us from the beginning of time, to share as one and to be one...one life, one love, one heart. I welcome you, _____, as my husband / wife, and I promise with God's help to be your faithful husband / wife, to love and serve you as Christ commands, as long as we both shall live."

♥ ♥ ♥ ♥

"_____, I give myself to you as your husband / wife, to join with you and be true to you with my whole being. My heart is open and my soul rejoices to God as we become one. I promise to love you for all the days of my life, in my waking and in my sleeping, in joy or sadness, so help me God."

♥ ♥ ♥ ♥

"I love you, _____, and before our God, our family and our friends, I take you to be my husband / wife and I give myself to you—all that I am, all that I have and all that I will ever be. Just as Jesus Christ has loved me with an unconditional love, so shall I love you. I will always seek to communicate with you in honesty and with total respect for your opinions, seeking your happiness and best interests in life. And just as God forgives me, so shall I forgive you and love you as I love myself. I promise to keep our love fresh, never allowing it to stagnate, seeking to express my love for you in some way every day. I hereby give myself to you, totally, unreservedly and eternally, for as long as we shall live together on this earth."

♥ ♥ ♥ ♥

Bride: "We are soul mates; I'm so blessed to have found you at last."

Groom: "Yes, we are soul mates, and my life is now complete because of you."

Bride: "Because of you, there is melody in my life."

Groom: "Because of you, my life is filled with song."

Bride: "I thank God for you, and I give myself freely to you as your wife."

Groom: "I praise God for you, as well, and I give myself freely to you as your husband."

Bride: "I have no doubts, no reservations."

Groom: "And I have none; in fact, I give my heart to you today with pure abandonment."

Bride: "My commitment to you is eternal."

Groom: "And mine to you, from this day forth, so help me God."

"I come to you today, before this company of witnesses, to join with you in holy matrimony, as your faithful husband / wife. I promise to be true to you always, forsaking all others, as I give you all that I am and all that I will ever be. May our marriage be protected by God's love and may no one ever disturb our union...May God bless our marriage."

♥ ♥ ♥ ♥

Bride: "God blessed me the day I found you."

Groom: "And you are God's indescribable gift to me."

Bride: "You give purpose to my life."

Groom: "And you make each day a special day for me."

Bride: "There is nothing more important in my life than your happiness; this is proof of my true love for you."

Groom: "And my true love for you is demonstrated by my promise to care for you always, putting you first in my life."

Bride: "I want to share my life with you; I want you there at my side to face all the joys and despairs of the future."

Groom: "I promise to be there for you always, to help you, comfort you, encourage you and lift you up, no matter what the circumstances."

Bride: "I give myself to you, wholly, with joy, to be your faithful wife and the mother of your children. Please accept my love."

Groom: "I give myself to you, wholly, with joy, to be your faithful husband and the father of our children. Please accept my love."

♥ ♥ ♥ ♥

Up close and personal

On July 29, 1995, my husband and I had the privilege of attending the wedding of Colleen Nelson and Joel Blomenkamp. What made this wedding so extra-special was not only that they wrote their own poignant, personalized wedding vows, but that they had waited seven long years, determined to graduate from college before getting married. They were high school sweethearts, of course, and graduated together from Biola University, she with a bachelor of arts degree in liberal studies; his was in social science. Here are the vows they wrote, memorized and flawlessly recited to each other:

Colleen: "Joel, I stand before you today, honored and excited as I am about to become your wife. I thank the Lord for the enduring and patient love He has given us these past seven years. You are a loving, gentle and kind man. You're devoted and committed to serving others and the Lord. You are the love of my life and I am so blessed with the gift of spending the rest of my life with you.

"As we become husband and wife today, I promise to love you with an unending and unconditional love. I will honor and respect you; comfort and cherish you. May I bring you good, not harm, all the days of my life. I will stand by you and submit to you as God guides us to do His will.

"I will be with you in sickness and in health, whether we are rich or poor, and during the times when we are filled with joy or when we are filled with sorrow. I will not leave you.

"Joel, I will be yours alone as long as God allows us to live."

Joel: "Today, I have come to commit my love to you. Although I come with a fallible love, I promise to strive to love you as Christ has loved the church. I promise to cherish you in times of joy and despair, to care for you when you are sick and in health, to hope with you now and forever, to protect you and not to harm you, to love you and to forsake all others.

"I promise to love you as scripture commands me to, 'for love is patient, love is kind. It does not envy, it does not boast, it is not proud. It is not rude, it is not self-seeking, it is not easily angered, it keeps no record of wrongs. Love does not delight in evil, but rejoices with the truth. It always protects, always hopes,

always perseveres. Where there are prophecies, they will cease; where there are tongues, they will be stilled; where there is knowledge, it will pass away, but love...love never fails. And now these three remain: Faith, Hope and Love, but the greatest of these is Love.'

"Although calamity and darkness may surround us, I promise to be here when you need me. Although the world values 'being in love,' I promise to love you even if the feelings of love go away. Before our friends and family, before you, and before my Lord and Savior, I commit these promises to you."

Joel and Colleen are presently teaching school in Southern California, and when I spoke to them recently on the telephone they sure sounded happy.

Vows for the bride and groom who are going into full-time Christian ministry

"_____, as we go forward from this, our wedding day, into God's service, I give you the love of my heart and I promise to be a loving and faithful husband / wife, with thanks to God whose gift of love has brought us together and lifted us up to serve Him together in joy and gladness. Our union is a holy union as we become one, husband and wife, joined together by God's ordinance of holy matrimony. How blessed we are to have found each other and God's holy will for our lives. I promise to love you, _____, to honor and cherish you, from this day forward. Our service may bring many hardships and disappointments, but together we will be strong

in the Lord and faithful to each other, upholding each
other in prayer, always ready to comfort and
encourage. Our service will bring many joys, as well,
and this, too, we will share in common praise and
thanksgiving to our Lord who has us always in the
palm of His hand."

"_____, God has called us to serve Him
together and as I take you today as my husband / wife,
my first priority is my own relationship with God, to
be right with Him and to have the assurance of being
in His will; I know this is the first priority in your life,
as well. But after my commitment to God comes my
total devotion to you as I become your wife / husband.
You have been blessed with many abilities and gifts
and I promise to encourage you as you develop these
God-given talents; I promise to support you in your
ministry as you seek to serve Him. I will pray for you
and encourage you in your Christian walk so that you
will be free to be all He wants you to be. I will love
you, care for you, sacrifice for you and be faithful to
you from this day forward and for all the years to
come. May God bless our marriage and our ministry
together."

♥ ♥ ♥ ♥

Vows based on a traditional Protestant prayer

"I thank the Almighty God, our heavenly Father, the
Fountain of all our joy, for giving you to me. I pledge
my sacred vow to walk with you in love, to rejoice in
the bond of marriage, to carry the inspiration of this
hour with me the rest of my life, whether there is joy or

*sorrow, whether there are pleasant days or trials. I
will be a comfort and a joy to you always, I will be
your counsel and strength as we walk together along
the pathway of life in faith, hope and love."*

Vows based on the Episcopalian declaration of intent

*"I vow to be your faithful husband / wife,
understanding that marriage is a lifelong union, and
not to be entered into lightly, for the purpose of mutual
fellowship, encouragement and understanding; for the
procreation of children and their physical and
spiritual nurture. I hereby give myself to you in this
cause with my sacred vow before God."*

Interfaith weddings

Interfaith weddings have become commonplace in our
country, naturally resulting in many variations of the traditional religious wedding vows. An interfaith service may
be conducted by a clergyperson sympathetic to the individual faiths of the bride and groom, or the service may be
purely ecumenical with two officiants, one representing the
bride, and one the groom. In some cases it isn't possible for
an interfaith marriage to be officially sanctioned at all. Orthodox and Conservative Jewish rabbis, for example, usually
refuse to officiate at a mixed marriage and the Roman
Catholic attitude is usually that, on a case-by-case basis, it
is possible for a Catholic to marry a non-Catholic, but only
under certain conditions. For example, in such a marriage
a Catholic groom may be required to promise, either in
writing or orally, that he will do all in his power to share
the Catholic faith with any children that may result from

the union; he must also promise that these children will be baptized and reared as Catholics.

There are multitudes of rules and restrictions within Protestant denominations as well. These rules not only vary from one denomination to the other, but from one congregation to another. For example, a divorced person usually may not be married within the Episcopal faith, except by special permission, and in order for a couple to be married in a Quaker wedding service, at least one of the couple must be a member of the Religious Society of Friends. The restrictions are so varied that it is always wise to set an appointment with the clergyperson of the particular church you have chosen before making further plans.

Here are several examples of interfaith wedding services and their vows:

Jewish-Christian

A typical Jewish-Christian wedding ceremony is conducted by co-officiants; here are the wedding vows used recently in one of these services:

> *"I, _____, take you, _____, to be my wedded wife / husband; and I promise and covenant, before God and these witnesses, to be your loving and faithful husband / wife, in plenty and in want, in joy and in sorrow, in sickness and in health, as long as we both shall live."*

Or this simpler version may also be used:

> *Officiant to the Bride / Groom: "Do you, _____, take _____ to be your lawfully wedded wife / husband, and do you promise to love, honor, and cherish her / him as long as you shall live / love?"*
>
> *Bride / Groom: "I do."*

Catholic-Non-Catholic

The wedding of a Catholic and a non-Catholic usually includes one of these vows:

> *"I, _____, take you, _____, to be my wife / husband. I promise to be true to you in good times and in bad, in sickness and in health. I will love you and honor you all the days of my life."*

or:

> *The Priest to the Groom / Bride: "_____, do you take _____ to be your wife / husband? Do you promise to be true to her / him in good times and in bad, in sickness and in health, to love him / her and honor him / her all the days of your life?"*
>
> *Groom / Bride: "I do."*

Catholic-Jewish

This type of wedding service is usually co-officiated by a Priest and a Rabbi and the wedding vows vary; consists of an Introduction (by the Priest or Rabbi); often the bride and groom compose their own vows or incorporate phrasings from the traditional Catholic and Jewish services. A common alternative is as follows:

> *"_____, I accept you as my wife / husband and call upon the Jewish and Christian communities to witness our union."*

Messianic Jew-Christian

This is the marriage of a Jew who believes in Yeshua (Jesus) and a gentile Christian. These ceremonies usually incorporate all the traditional Jewish marriage rituals and are conducted by a rabbi; they differ from the Orthodox, Conservative or Reformed Jewish marriage ceremonies, however, because of the couple's belief that Yeshua, Jesus of Nazareth, is the Messiah and the King of the Jews.

Up close and personal

I am acquainted with such a couple, Andrew and Karen Goldberg, members of the Ahavat Zion Messianic Synagogue in Beverly Hills, California, who were married on June 25, 1995 at The Chateau Bradbury in Duarte, California by their rabbi, Rabbi Stuart Dauermann. Many Messianic Jewish Synagogues throughout the United States conduct their services on the Sabbath, according to Jewish tradition.

Andrew and Karen have a fascinating love story: They first met over the campus computer bulletin board when they both attended the University of Southern California. They communicated via their computers for two years before finally meeting in person. Karen is now an instructional designer for Crane Morley and Andrew plans to teach, having just graduated from California State University, Long Beach, in December 1995 with a degree in math.

They have kindly provided me with a copy of their rabbi's notes for the wedding sermon, as well as the details of their service, including the wording for the exchange of their rings and vows and the Seven Blessings that were read in both Hebrew and English.

Rabbi Dauermann (to Andrew): "Andrew Neil, son of Karl and Patricia Goldberg, may your house and the household of G-d increase. Do you attest, that after prayer and due consideration to know the will of G-d for your life, that the G-d of Israel, Blessed be He, has moved you to take this woman at your side to be your bride?"

Andrew: "I do."

Rabbi Dauermann: "Do you promise to uphold her, devoting yourself to her welfare and nurture, encouraging her in her walk with G-d, conscious that by her service to G-d, He would have her submit herself to you as her husband in love and faith?"

Andrew: "I do."

Rabbi Dauermann: "What token do you offer as a sign or symbol of your love for her in the sight of G-d? Place the ring on her finger and repeat after me:

'Harei at mikudeshet li'	*'With this ring'*
'B'taba'aat zu'	*'you are consecrated to me'*
'k'da'at Elohei Yisrael'	*'according to the ordinance of G-d of Israel.' "*

Rabbi Dauermann (to Karen): "Karen Ann, daughter of Larry Birch and Judy Chambers, may the L-rd make you like Sarah and Rebekkah, like Rachael and Leah. Do you attest that after prayer and due consideration to know the will of G-d for your life, that the G-d of Israel, Blessed by He, has moved you join your life to that of this man at your side to be his bride?"

Karen: "I do."

Rabbi Dauermann: "Do you promise to honor him as your husband, submitting to him, and helping him in every way to grow in submission to the will of G-d?"

Karen: "I do."

Rabbi Dauermann: "What token do you offer as a sign or symbol of your love for him in the sight of G-d? Place the ring on his finger and repeat after me:

'Harei at mikudeshet li'	*'With this ring'*
'B'taba'aat zu'	*'you are consecrated to me'*
'k'da'at Elohei Yisrael'	*'according to the ordinance of G-d of Israel.'*

"The Seven Blessings:

"You Abound in Blessings, Adonai our G-d, who creates the fruit of the vine.

"You Abound in Blessings, Adonai our G-d, You created all things for Your glory.

"You Abound in Blessings, Adonai our G-d, You created humanity.

"You Abound in Blessings, Adonai our G-d, You made humankind in Your image, after Your likeness, and You prepared from us a perpetual relationship. You Abound in Blessings, Adonai our G-d, You created humanity.

"May she who was barren rejoice when her children are united in her midst in joy. You Abound in Blessings, Adonai our G-d, who makes Zion rejoice with her children.

"You make these beloved companions greatly rejoice even as You rejoiced in Your creation in the Garden of Eden as of old. You Abound in Blessings, Adonai our G-d, who makes the bridegroom and bride to rejoice.

"You Abound in Blessings, Adonai our G-d, who created joy and gladness, bridegroom and bride, mirth and exultation, pleasure and delight, love, fellowship, peace and friendship. Soon may there be heard in the cities of Judah and in the streets of Jerusalem, the voice of joy and gladness, the voice of the bridegroom and the voice of the bride, the jubilant voice of the bridegrooms from their canopies and of youths from their feast of song as the Messiah who is the eternal bridegroom to all who trust Him returns to gather Jacob's children from every corner of the earth. You Abound in Blessings, Adonai our G-d, You make the bridegroom rejoice with the bride."

Note: These Seven Blessings are almost identical to the traditional Seven Blessings already given in Chapter 1 in the section on Jewish ceremonies; the important difference is the mention of the Messiah in the seventh blessing where He is referred to as the "eternal bridegroom to all who trust Him."

Chapter 8

Ring Vows

The wedding ring is seen as a seal upon the wedding vow, a symbol of the couple's lifetime commitment to one another. It is also seen by some to be a religious symbol of the holiness and sacredness of marriage, as ordained by God. This chapter contains a variety of ring vows, some traditional, and many, nontraditional, since it has become popular for the bride and groom to write their own personalized ring vows, as well as the wedding vows themselves.

Jewish

Rabbi (addressing the bridegroom): "Then, do you, _____, put this ring upon the finger of your bride and say to her: 'Be thou consecrated to me, as my wife, by this ring, according to the Law of Moses and of Israel.'"

The Rabbi then asks the bride to repeat the following:

"May this ring I receive from thee be a token of my having become thy wife according to the Law of Moses and of Israel."

If two rings are used, the bride may say:

"This ring is a symbol that thou art my husband in accordance with the Law of Moses and Israel."

Catholic

The priest blesses the rings:

"Blessing of the Wedding Rings
Our help is in the name of the Lord.
Who made heaven and earth.
O Lord, hear my prayer.
And let my cry come unto Thee.
The Lord be with you.
And with your spirit."

Priest (to the couple): "Now that you have sealed a truly Christian marriage, give these wedding rings to each other, saying after me:"

Groom (addressing his bride): "In the name of the Father, and of the Son, and of the Holy Spirit. Take and wear this ring as a pledge of my fidelity."

Bride (addressing her bridegroom): "In the name of the Father, and of the Son, and of the Holy Spirit. Take and wear this ring as a pledge of my fidelity."

American Lutheran

"I give you this ring as a sign of my love and faithfulness."

Episcopalian

Groom / bride: "_____, I give you this ring as a symbol of my vow, and with all that I am, and all that I have, I honor you, in the Name of the Father, and of the Son, and of the Holy Spirit (or 'in the Name of God')."

Presbyterian

Groom / bride: "This ring I give you, in token and pledge, of our constant faith, and abiding love."

or:

"With this ring I thee wed, in the name of the Father, and of the Son, and of the Holy Spirit. Amen."

Methodist

Groom / bride: "_____, I give you this ring as a sign of my vow, and with all that I am, and all that I have, I honor you."

♥ ♥ ♥ ♥

United Church of Christ

"This ring I give you in token of my faithfulness and love, and as a pledge to honor you with my whole being and to share with you my worldly goods."

or:

"I give you this ring in token of the covenant made today between us; in the name of the Father, and of the Son, and of the Holy Spirit."

United Church of Canada

"_____, I give you this ring that you may wear it as a symbol of our marriage."

Unitarian/Universalist

The minister repeats these words as the rings are exchanged between the bride and groom:

"As a token of mutual fidelity and affection the ring(s) are now given and received."

The bride and groom, if they wish, may repeat their own ring vows:

"With this ring, I wed you and pledge you my love now and forever."

or:

"Be consecrated to me, with this ring, as my wife/husband in accordance with the faith of our loved ones."

Catholic-Non-Catholic

"_____, *take this ring as a sign of my love and fidelity. In the name of the Father, and of the Son, and of the Holy Spirit.*"

Jewish-Christian

"*Be thou consecrated unto me with this ring as my wife / husband, according to the faith of God and humanity.*"

Nondenominational

Groom: "I offer you this ring as a sign of my love and fidelity. It will always be a symbol of the vows which have made us husband and wife here this morning."

Bride: "I accept this ring as a symbol of our love and wear it proudly as your wife."

"*Dear _____, with this ring I thee wed, and by it be thou consecrated unto me, as my wedded wife / husband according to the laws of God and of man.*"

"*With this ring I wed you and pledge my faithful love. I take you as my husband / wife and pledge to share*

my life openly with you, to speak the truth to you in love. I promise to honor and tenderly care for you, to cherish and encourage your fulfillment as an individual through all the changes of our lives."

Minister: *"Now, may I have a token of your sincerity that you will keep these vows?"*

(The best man gives the bride's ring to the minister who then holds it up and says:)

"From the beginning of time, the ring has symbolized many kinds of human relationships. Kings wore them to express their imperial authority; friends exchanged them as expressions of their good will; high school and college graduates wore them as expressions of their school loyalties. This simple band of gold, however, has come to its highest significance as a symbol of a marriage relationship. Wearing it bears witness to your marital fidelity."

(The minister hands the bride's ring to the groom and instructs him to place it on her finger.)

Minister (to the groom): *"Do you, _____, give this ring to _____ as a token of your love for her?"*

Groom: *"I do."*

Minister (to the bride): *"Will you, _____, take this ring from _____ as a token of his love for you and will you wear it as an expression of your love for him?"*

Bride: *"I will."*

(The minister takes the groom's ring from the maid or matron of honor or from the ring bearer and gives it to the bride, instructing her to place it on the groom's finger.)

Minister (to the bride): "Do you, _____, give this ring to _____ as an expression of your love for him?"

Bride: "I do."

Minister (to the groom): "Will you, _____, take this ring from _____ as a token of her love for you and will you wear it as an expression of your love for her?"

Groom: "I will."

"I bring this ring as a symbol of my love and fidelity as your husband / wife, and as I slide it onto your finger, I commit my very heart and soul to you, my dear husband / wife, and I ask you to wear it as a reminder of the vows we have taken today."

"With this ring I thee wed, in the Name of God. Amen."

"With this ring I wed thee and I accept thee as my husband / wife; I take thee as my partner in life and I hereby endow thee with all my worldly goods."

♥ ♥ ♥ ♥

"May this ring be a permanent reminder of our holy promises and steadfast love, through Jesus Christ our Lord. Amen."

"_____, this ring is the sign of my love and faithfulness, and I give it to you in the name of the Father, the Son and the Holy Spirit. Amen."

"Thou art my beloved and I give thee this ring as a visible reminder to you and all who see it that my love for you is constant and eternal."

"You are my life, my love, my best friend and with this ring I wed thee; may it be a reminder of my love and the sacred commitment I have made here today."

"When we were in high school, I gave you my class ring and you wore it on a chain around your neck to show the world that we were going steady. But today I give you something much more precious: a wedding ring; may it be a sign to all who see it that we're going steady for the rest of our lives and that you belong to me alone."

"As this ring encircles your finger from this day forward, year in and year out, so will my love forever encircle you. Wear this ring as a symbol of this love."

"With this ring I seal the commitment I have made to you today; may you wear it proudly as my wife/ husband."

"_____, take this ring as a seal upon the marriage vows I have spoken and, as you wear it, may it be a reminder of how much I love you, not only on this precious day, but every single day of your life."

"This ring is the visible evidence of our invisible love; it symbolizes the joining of our spirits in sacred holy matrimony."

"As I place this ring on your finger, its perfect symmetry is a symbol of our perfect love. It has no beginning and no ending, a symbol of the eternal commitment we have made to each other today."

*"This ring is round and hath no end,
So is my love unto my friend."*

16th-century verse

"Our love is even more precious than this diamond (or whatever stone the bride wears in her engagement

ring), *and more enduring than this band of gold, but I place this band on your finger as a symbol of our love and the vows we have spoken here today."*

"Just as this ring is made from precious metal, sturdy and strong, so will our marriage be: a precious commitment to each other that remains sturdy and strong until death do us part."

"This ring is enduring evidence of my enduring love and its purity is a symbol of the sacredness of our vows."

"Today we are on a mountaintop; everything is good and happy and right. But someday there will be valleys as well, and as we walk through those valleys together, may this ring be a reminder of this mountaintop experience, and the vows we have made this day."

"Just as our love is shining and pure, so is this golden wedding ring, an emblem of the lifelong commitment I have made to you this day."

"With this ring I wed you—not only for today, our wedding day, so all may see its golden glow; but for all our tomorrows, until death do us part. Wear it as a

*sign of my love for you and a notice to the world that
you have chosen me to be your husband / wife."*

*"_____, with this ring I wed you; with my
body I worship you, and with all my worldly goods I
endow you."*

*"As a sign of my commitment and the desire of my
heart, I give you this ring. May it always be a
reminder that I have chosen you above all other
women / men and that, from this day forward, you are
my wife / husband."*

*Minister: "I hold in my hand two beautiful rings,
symbolic of a binding contract, to be given and
received as bonds of never-ending love and devoted
friendship, circles of life and circles of love."*

(The minister hands one of the rings to the groom who
places it on his bride's finger.)

*Groom: "With this ring I wed thee and offer it as a
symbol of our everlasting love."*

(The minister hands the other ring to the bride who places
it on her groom's finger.)

*Bride: "With this ring I wed thee and offer it as a
symbol of our everlasting love."*

Up close and personal

I'm sure you remember the story in Chapter 2 of Bill and Kathy who fell in love at first sight at an engagement party for their mutual friend and were married under the wet tent in Colorado. Here are their ring vows:

Minister: "The perfect circle of a ring symbolizes eternity, while gold is a symbol of all that is pure and holy. As you give these rings to each other, our prayer is that your love for each other will be as eternal and everlasting as these rings. William, place this ring on Kathryn's finger and repeat after me:"

Bill (repeating after the minister): "Kathryn, with this ring, I symbolize our union as husband and wife—for today, tomorrow, and all the years to come. Please wear it as a reminder of our deep and abiding love."

Minister: "Kathryn, place this ring on William's finger and repeat after me:"

Kathryn (repeating after the minister): "William, I also give you this ring as a symbol of our union as husband and wife—for today, tomorrow and all the years to come. Please wear it as a reminder of our deep and abiding love."

♥ ♥ ♥ ♥

"_____, I give you this ring as a symbol, not only of my love for you and my promise to be your faithful husband / wife, but as a reminder that God is also part of our marriage, to be honored and praised every day of our lives."

♥ ♥ ♥ ♥

"_____, *whenever the world sees this ring on your finger, it will be a symbol of my love for you and that, although I may not be present with you at that moment, I am always faithful to you, honoring you and cherishing you as my husband / wife."*

"This wedding band is a perfect circle of precious metal that symbolizes a man's kingdom and his earthly possessions, and as I place this ring on your finger, I entrust you with my kingdom and possessions. When you look at this ring in the years to come, may it remind you of my vows to you this day and may you always feel encircled by my love, just as this band encircles your finger."

"_____, *I give you this ring as a symbol of my love for you. Let it remind you always, as it circles your finger, of my eternal love, surrounding you and enfolding you day and night."*

"You are my beloved bride / bridegroom and I marry you today with this ring as I give you my heart, my body and the very breath of my soul."

"Just as this gold band wraps endlessly around your finger, so shall my love always wrap around the very breath of your soul; may it be a reminder of the sacred vows I have spoken this day."

Minister (to the bride and groom): "I will ask you now to seal the vows which you have just made by the giving and receiving of rings. Let us remember that the circle is the emblem of eternity and it is our prayer that your love and happiness will be as unending as the rings which you exchange."

Minister (to the groom): "_____, do you have a token of your love?"

Groom: "Yes, a ring."

(The best man gives the ring to the minister; the minister gives it to the groom; the groom places it on his bride's finger and then repeats after the minister:)

"This ring I give thee, in token and pledge, of our constant faith, and abiding love."

Minister (to the bride): "_____, do you have a token of your love?"

Bride: "Yes, a ring."

(The maid or matron of honor gives the ring to the minister; the minister gives it to the bride; the bride then places it on the finger of the groom and repeats after the minister:)

"This ring I give thee, in token and pledge, of our constant faith, and abiding love."

*"Go little ring to that same sweet
That hath my heart in her domain..."*

Geoffrey Chaucer

♥ ♥ ♥ ♥

Ring vows with the covenant of salt

Minister: "For centuries, rings have symbolized the sealing of covenants and commitments."

(The best man gives the bride's ring to the minister who then holds it up and says:)

"This ring is a circle; it symbolizes the continuity of the marriage bond—a marriage for as long as you both shall live."

(The minister hands the bride's ring to the groom and instructs him to place it on her finger.)

Minister (to the groom): "Do you, _____, give this ring to _____ as a token of your love for her?"

Groom: "I do."

Minister: "Then, as a ceaseless reminder of this hour and of the vows you have taken, _____, place this ring on the hand of your bride and repeat after me:"

Groom (repeating after the minister): "With this ring I thee wed, with loyal love I thee endow, and all my worldly goods with thee I share, in the name of the Father and the Son and the Holy Spirit. Amen."

(The minister takes the groom's ring from the maid or matron of honor or from the ring bearer and holds it up.)

Minister: "This ring has not always been the beautiful gold that we see here today. It came from the ground as rough ore—that ore had to be tried by a refiner fire—to drive away the impurities; now only the precious gold remains. May this ring be a symbol of difficult times. Problems will come in your marriage, but they can be like the refiner fire that drives away the impurities—leaving only the precious gold of your love, a love that shall grow more precious and beautiful as years pass by."

(The minister hands the ring to the bride.)

Minister (to the bride): "Do you, _____, give this ring to _____ as an expression of your love for him?"

Bride: "I do."

Minister (to the groom): "Will you, _____, take this ring from _____ as a token of her love for you and will you wear it as an expression of your love for her?"

Groom: "I will."

Minister (to the bride): "Then, as a ceaseless reminder of this hour and of the vows you have taken, _____, place this ring on the hand of your groom and repeat after me."

Bride (repeating after the minister): "With this ring I thee wed; intreat me not to leave thee or to return from following after thee, for whither thou goest I will go and where thou lodgest I will lodge: thy people shall be my people and thy God my God."

Minister (to the bride and groom): "_____ and _____, you have just sealed your covenant by the giving and receiving of rings, and this covenant is a relationship agreement between two parties who agree that they will commit themselves to one another for the keeping of their partnership throughout their lives. The most beautiful example of this partnership is the marriage relationship. You have committed here today to share the rest of your lives with each other and that nothing, save death, will ever cause you to part. You entered this relationship as two distinct individuals, but from this day forth your lives will be so totally melded together that you will never be able to separate.

"This covenant relationship is symbolized through the pouring of these two individual bags of salt—one representing you, _____, and all that you were, all that you are and all that you will ever be, and the other representing you, _____, and all that you were and all that you are, and all that you will ever be. As these two bags of salt are poured into the third bag, the individual bags of salt will no longer exist, but will be joined together as one. Just as these grains of salt can never separated and poured again into the individual bags, so will your marriage be. Far more important than your individuality is now the reality that you are no longer two, but one, never to be separated one from the other."

(The bride and groom each empties his/her individual bag of salt into a third bag.)

"_____ and _____, we have heard your vows and you've symbolized your union by pledging your lives to each other, exchanging rings and through the Covenant of Salt. So, by the authority of God's word and the state of _____, as a minister of the Gospel, I now pronounce you husband and wife."

Up close and personal

You may remember another love story from an earlier chapter, that of Eric Wood and Kimberly Gray. Here are the personalized ring vows they wrote for their ceremony:

Minister: "The exchanging of rings has great meaning to Eric and Kimberly. These rings that they have chosen are engraved with a repeating pattern that, like the rings themselves, have no beginning and no end. Neither Kimberly nor Eric can remember when their love began, yet both can say it will have no end. By exchanging rings, Kimberly and Eric can show to each other and to all the love that they share."

Kimberly (repeating after the minister as she places the ring on Eric's finger): "Eric, I give you this ring as a sign to you and to all the love I carry only for you. I give it knowing that our love is in constant need of encouragement, yet is a constant in our lives. With patience, understanding, and communication, it will continue to grow. Accept this ring, knowing it comes from my heart and soul. Take it and wear it, that all who see it may know that I love you."

Eric (repeating after the minister as he places the ring on Kimberly's finger): "Kimberly, I give you this ring as a sign to you and to all of the love that I carry only for you. I give it, knowing that our love is in constant need of encouragement, yet is a constant in our lives. With patience, understanding, and communication, it will continue to grow. Accept this ring, knowing that it comes from my heart and soul. Take it and wear it, that all who see it may know that I love you."

Reaffirmation service

"We have lived and loved as we promised long ago in the presence of God, and our past and our future are a circle unbroken...like this ring, with which I renew my pledge to you of never ending devotion."

"With this ring I reaffirm my love for you, a love refined in the crucible of our togetherness. Wear it as my prayer of thanksgiving and of my hopes for all our tomorrows."

"First came the engagement ring, a promise of our wedding yet to come. Then came the gold band I placed on your finger on our wedding day when I promised to love you and cherish you until the end of my days. Now comes this ring of renewal, celebrating our ____ precious years of married life together and the joyous years yet to come. With this ring I reaffirm my love for you."

Chapter 9

Vows Inspired by the Classics

Many couples take phrasings from classical writings and incorporate them into their wedding vows. This works especially well for a formal or period costume wedding. In this chapter I have gathered a sampling of some of the more popular selections. As you read through these selections, keep in mind that you may use one in its entirety, combine it with other writings or ferret out specific phrases that can be incorporated into your own vows.

Let me not to the marriage of true minds
Admit impediments. Love is not love
Which alters when it alteration finds,

Or bends with the remover to remove:
O, no! It is an ever-fix'd mark,
That looks on tempests and is never shaken;
It is the star to every wandering bark,
Whose worth's unknown, although his height be
taken.
Love's not Time's fool, though rosy lips and cheeks
Within his bending sickle's compass come;
Love alters not with his brief hours and weeks,
But bears it out even to the edge of doom.
If this be error and upon me prov'd,
I never writ, nor no man ever lov'd.

Shakespearean sonnet 116

Shall I compare thee to a summer's day?
Thou art more lovely and more temperate...
When in eternal lines to time thou grow'st
So long as men can breathe or eyes can see,
So long lives this, and this gives life to thee.

Shakespearean sonnet 18

"Then happy I that love and am beloved
Where I may not remove nor be removed."

Shakespearean sonnet 25

"But here's the joy: my friend and I are one...
Then she loves but me alone!"

Shakespearean sonnet 42

Thy love is better than high birth to me,
Richer than wealth, prouder than garments' cost,
Of more delight than hawks or horses be;
And, having thee, of all men's pride I boast...

Shakespearean sonnet 91

"Love cometh like sunshine after rain."

Shakespeare

"Look down you gods, and on this couple drop a
blessed crown."

Shakespeare

If you enjoy Shakespeare, go to your library and check out
the volume that contains all of his sonnets.

Love one another, but make not a bond of love:
Let it rather be a moving sea between the shores of
your souls.
Fill each other's cup but drink not from one cup.
Give one another of your bread but eat not from the
same loaf.

*Sing and dance together and be joyous, but let each
one of you be alone,
Even as the strings of a lute are alone though they
quiver with the same music.
Give your hearts, but not into each other's keeping.
For only the hand of Life can contain your hearts.
And stand together yet not too near together:
For the pillars of the temple stand apart,
And the oak tree and the cypress grow not in each
other's shadow.*

Kahlil Gibran

*"Love gives naught but itself and takes naught but
from itself. Love possesses not nor would it be
possessed; for love is sufficient unto love."*

Kahlil Gibran

*"Marriage is the golden ring in a chain whose
beginning is a glance and whose ending is Eternity."*

Kahlil Gibran

*"Sensual pleasure passes and vanishes in the twinkling
of an eye, but the friendship between us, the mutual
confidence, the delights of the heart, the enchantment of
the soul, these things do not perish and can never be
destroyed. I shall love you until I die."*

Voltaire

"It is the man and woman united that makes the complete human being. Separate she lacks his force of body and strength of reason; he her softness, sensibility and acute discernment. Together they are most likely to succeed in the world."

Benjamin Franklin

"There is no more lovely, friendly and charming relationship, communion or company than a good marriage."

Martin Luther

O my Luve's like a red, red rose
That's newly sprung in June;
O my Luve's like the melodie
That's sweetly played in tune.
As fair art thou, my bonnie lass,
So deep in luve am I;
And I will luve thee still, my dear,
Till a' the seas gang dry.

Robert Burns

"Tonight is a night of union and also of scattering of the stars,
for a bride is coming from the sky: the full moon.
The sky is an astrolabe, and the Law is Love."

From "Persian Love Poem" by Jalal Al-Din Rumi

Come live with me, and be my love,
And we will some new pleasures prove
Of golden sands, and crystal brooks,
With silken lines, and silver hooks

John Donne

"To get the full value of joy, you must have someone to divide it with."

Mark Twain

"Better is a heart full of love, than a mind filled with knowledge."

Charles Dickens

"Friendship is a union of spirits, a marriage of hearts, and the bond of virtue."

William Penn

"...and yet even while I was exulting in my solitude I became aware of a strange lack. I wished a companion to lie near me in the starlight, silent and not moving, but ever within touch. For there is a fellowship more quiet even than solitude, and which, rightly understood, is solitude made perfect. And to

*live...with the woman a man loves is of all lives the
most complete and free."*

Robert Louis Stevenson, from "A Night
Among the Pines"

*Go seek her out all courteously,
And say I come,
Wind of spices whose song is ever
Epithalamium.
O hurry over the dark lands
And run upon the sea
For seas and land shall not divide us
My love and me.
Now, wind, of your good courtesy
I pray you go,
And come into her little garden
And sing at her window;
Singing: The bridal wind is blowing
For Love is at his noon;
And soon will your true love be with you,
Soon, O soon.*

James Joyce from his poem XIII, *Chamber Music*

*Oh, hasten not this loving act,
Rapture where self and not-self meet;
My life has been the awaiting you,
Your footfall was my own heart's beat.*

Paul Valery

♥ ♥ ♥ ♥

When our two souls stand up erect and strong,
Face to face, silent, drawing nigh and nigher,
Until the lengthening wings break into fire
At either curved point,—what bitter wrong
Can the earth do us, that we should not long
Be here contented! Think. In mounting higher,
The angels would press on us and aspire
To drop some golden orb of perfect song
Into our deep, dear silence. Let us stay
Rather on earth, Beloved—where the unfit
contrarious moods of men recoil away
And isolate pure spirits, and permit
A place to stand and love in for a day...

How do I love thee? Let me count the ways.
I love thee to the depth and breadth and height
My soul can reach, when feeling out of sight
For the ends of Being and ideal Grace.
I love thee to the level of everyday's
Most quiet need, by sun and candle-light.
I love thee freely, as men strive for Right;
I love thee purely, as they turn from Praise.
I love thee with the passion put to use
In my old griefs, and with my childhood's faith.
I love thee with a love I seemed to lose
With my lost saints,—I love thee with the breath,
Smiles, tears, of all my life!—and, if God choose,
I shall but love thee better after death.

Inspired by the words of Elizabeth Barrett
Browning, from *Sonnets from the Portuguese*

Vows based on scripture

Genesis 2:21-24

"And the Lord God caused a deep sleep to fall upon Adam, and he slept: and he took one of his ribs, and closed up the flesh instead thereof; and the rib, which the Lord God had taken from man, made he a woman, and brought her unto the man. And Adam said, This is now bone of my bones, and flesh of my flesh: she shall be called Woman, because she was taken out of Man. Therefore shall a man leave his father and his mother and shall cleave unto his wife: and they shall be one flesh. And so, just as Eve was formed from Adam's rib, not from his head as to rule him, or from his foot to be stepped on, but from his side, to be a helpmate, a partner in life, you have been given to me by God, _____, to be my partner as we walk side by side through life together and I hereby vow before God and these witnesses to be a true and faithful husband to you, always nurturing, comforting and supporting, loving you until I live no more."

Mark 10:6-9

"But from the beginning of the creation God made them male and female. For this cause shall a man leave his father and mother, and cleave to his wife; and they twain shall be one flesh: so then they are no more twain, but one flesh. What therefore God hath joined together, let not man put asunder. _____, as we are united in marriage this day, we shall also cleave to each other, no longer twain, but becoming one flesh, and no forces on earth can ever tear us apart. I pledge my love to you eternally until death parts us."

Ecclesiastes 4:9-12

"Two are better than one; because they have a good reward for their labour. For if they fall, the one will lift up his fellow; but woe to him that is alone when he falleth; for he hath not another to help him up. Again, if two lie together, then they have heat; but how can one be warm alone? And if one prevail against him, two shall withstand him; and a threefold cord is not quickly broken."

"_____, I promise, as the scripture says, to stand by your side, always ready to help you up; I promise to lie by your side, always ready to warm you; and I promise to prevail with you, always ready to withstand the hardships of this world. Our marriage bond will be strong, unbreakable, eternal, and I pledge this to you before these witnesses, so help me God."

Ruth 1:16-17

Ruth said:
"Entreat me not to leave thee,
Or to return from following after thee:
For wither thou goest, I will go,
And where thou lodgest, I will lodge.
Thy people shall be my people,
And thy God my God.
Where thou diest, will I die,
And there will I be buried.
The Lord do so to me, and more also,
If ought but death part thee and me."

Ephesians 5:28-33

*"So ought men to love their wives as their own bodies.
He that loveth his wife loveth himself. For no man
ever yet hated his own flesh; but nourisheth and
cherisheth it, even as the Lord the church: For we are
members of his body, of his flesh, and of his bones.
For this cause shall a man leave his father and
mother, and shall be joined unto his wife, and the two
shall become one flesh. This is a great mystery: but I
speak concerning Christ and the church. Nevertheless
let every one of you in particular so love his wife even
as himself; and the wife see that she reverence her
husband."*

♥ ♥ ♥ ♥

Song of Solomon 2:10-17

*"My beloved spake, and said unto me, Rise up, my
love, my fair one, and come away. For, lo, the winter
is past, the rain is over and gone; The flowers appear
on the earth; the time of the singing of birds is come,
and the voice of the turtle is heard in our land; The fig
tree putteth forth her green figs, and the vines with the
tender grape give a good smell. Arise, my love, my fair
one, and come away. O my dove, that art in the clefts
of the rock, in the secret places of the stairs, let me see
thy countenance, let me hear thy voice; for sweet is thy
voice, and thy countenance is comely. Take us the
foxes, the little foxes, that spoil the vines; for our vines
have tender grapes. My beloved is mine, and I am his:
he feedeth among the lilies. Until the day break, and
the shadows flee away, turn, my beloved, and be thou
like a roe or a young hart upon the mountains of
Bether."*

Here are other portions of scripture you may wish to consider:

Hebrews 13:4
Matthew 19:4-6
John 2:1-11
I John 4:7-19
Song of Solomon 7:11-12, 8:6b-7
Isaiah 43:1-5, 54:10, 60:19-22

Matthew 22:35-40
Romans 12:1-2, 9-18
Colossians 3:12-13
Proverbs 3:3-6
I Peter 3:7
Ephesians 4:1-4, 5:1-2

Old Indian wedding verses

"Now we feel no rain, for each of us will be shelter to the other. Now we will feel no cold, for each of us will be warmth to the other. Now there is no loneliness for us. Now we are two bodies, but only one life. We go now to our dwelling place, to enter into the days of our togetherness. May our days be good and long upon this earth."

Based on an Apache Indian prayer

"Fair is the white star of twilight, and the sky clearer at the day's end; but she is fairer, and she is dearer, She, my heart's friend.

Fair is the white star of twilight, and the moon roving to the sky's end; but she is fairer, better worth loving, She, my heart's friend."

Traditional Shoshone Indian love poem

"Oh, I am thinking
Oh, I am thinking
I have found my lover.
Oh, I think it is so."

Traditional Chippewa Indian poem of betrothal

"I know not whether thou has been absent:
I lie down with thee, I rise up with thee,
In my dreams thou art with me.
If my eardrops tremble in my ears,
I know it is thou moving within my heart."

Old Aztec Indian wedding poem

"O Morning Star! When you look down upon us, give
us peace and refreshing sleep. Great Spirit! Bless our
children, friends, and visitors through a happy life.
May our trails lie straight and level before us. Let us
live to be old. We are all your children and ask these
things with good hearts."

Traditional wedding prayer of the Great Plains Indian

"You are my husband/wife
My feet shall run because of you.
My feet, dance because of you.
My eyes, see because of you.
My mind, think because of you.
And I shall love because of you."

Old Eskimo Indian wedding vow

Classical vows for the reaffirmation service

If you are planning a formal reaffirmation service, you may wish to incorporate classical writings into your reaffirmation vows, drawing from Elizabeth Barrett Browning's letters, for example, or from the Bible or Shakespeare's many writings. Shakespeare's sonnets work especially well, in fact, and here are several of them that may be used in their entirety, if so desired. You and your spouse may alternate lines, if you wish, or you may each recite your own sonnet.

Shall I compare thee to a summer's day?
Thou art more lovely and more temperate.
Rough winds do shake the darling buds of May,
And summer's lease hath all too short a date.
And often is his gold complexion dimmed;
And every fair from fair sometime declines,
By chance or nature's changing course untrimmed.
But thy eternal summer shall not fade,
Nor lose possession of that fair thou ow'st,
Nor shall Death brag thou wand'rest in his shade,
When in eternal lines to time thou grow'st.
So long as men can breathe or eyes can see,
So long lives this, and this gives life to thee.

Shakespearean sonnet 18

Devouring Time, blunt thou the lion's paws,
And make the earth devour her own sweet brood;
Pluck the keen teeth from the fierce tiger's jaws,
And burn the long-lived phoenix in her blood;
Make glad and sorry seasons as thou fleet'st,

And do whate'er thou wilt, swift-footed Time,
To the wide world and all her fading sweets.
But I forbid thee one most heinous crime:
O, carve not with thy hours my love's fair brow,
Nor draw no lines there with thine antique pen;
Him in thy course untainted do allow
For beauty's pattern to succeeding men.
Yet do thy worst, Old Time; despite thy wrong,
My love shall in my verse ever live young.

Shakespearean sonnet 19

To me, fair friend, you never can be old,
For as you were when first your eye I eyed,
Such seems your beauty still. Three winters cold
Have from the forests shook three summers' pride,
Three beauteous springs to yellow autumn turned
In process of the seasons have I seen,
Three April perfumes in three hot Junes burned,
Since first I saw you fresh, which yet are green.
Ah, yet doth beauty, like a dial hand,
Steal from his figure, and no pace perceived;
So your sweet hue, which methinks still doth stand,
Hath motion, and mine eye may be deceived;
For fear of which, hear this, thou age unbred:
Ere you were born was beauty's summer dead.

Shakespearean sonnet 104

Those lines that I before have writ do lie,
Even those that said I could not love you dearer.
Yet then my judgement knew no reason why
My most full flame should afterwards burn clearer.
But reckoning Time, whose millioned accidents
Creep in 'twixt vows and change decrees of kings,
Tan sacred beauty, blunt the sharp'st intents,
Divert strong minds to th' course of alt'ring things—
Alas, why, fearing of Time's tyranny,
Might I not then say 'Now I love you best,'
When I was certain o'er incertainty,
Crowning the present, doubting of the rest?
Love is a babe; then might I not say so,
To give full growth to that which still doth grow.

Shakespearean sonnet 115

Shakespeare wrote 154 sonnets, all of which are available in a single volume at your local library. You will enjoy perusing through them, perhaps selecting a line or phrase here and there. Be sure to read Sonnets 15, 25, 76, 88 and 91, all of which offer lovely phrasings for your consideration. Who knows? They may even inspire you to wax eloquent and compose an original sonnet of your very own!

Another source of inspiration are the writings of Kahlil Gibran, including his love letters to Mary Haskell, the great love of his adult life. Here are excerpts from some of these letters that will work well for your affirmation vows:

"The most wonderful thing, Mary, is that you and I are always walking together, hand in hand, in a strangely beautiful world, unknown to other people. Love says, you are myself.

"You have the great gift of understanding, beloved Mary. You are a life-giver, Mary. My knowing you is the greatest thing in my days and nights, a miracle. That which is between us is like the Absolute in Life—everchanging, evergrowing. You and I, Mary, understand each other's larger self: and that to me is the most wonderful thing in life.

"Mary, you are the only person in the world with whom I feel wholly at home. The bond between you and me is greater than either of us knows. Between us the bond can't be broken. May Life sing in your heart, and may Life keep you in her most sacred heart.

"I shall love you to eternity. I loved you long before we met in this flesh. I knew that when I first saw you. It was destiny...nothing can shake us apart...I can't and God himself can't.

"The relation between you and me is the most beautiful thing in my life: It is eternal. Mary, I am always asking much of you, and like life itself you always give much. May God bless you for all that you do for me...may God love you and keep you near His heart."

Kahlil Gibran

John Keats' writings offer beautiful phrasings for reaffirmation vows, including these:

"July 1, 1819

...for myself I know not how to express my devotion to so fair a form: I want a brighter word than bright, a fairer word than fair. I almost wish we were butterflies and liv'd but three summer days—three such days with you I could fill with more delight than fifty common years could ever contain..."

John Keats

"March 1820

...my dear Girl I love you ever and ever and without reserve. The more I have known you the more have I lov'd. In every way—even my jealousies have been agonies of Love, in the hottest fit I ever had I would have died for you. I have vex'd you too much. But for Love! Can I help it? You are always new. The last of your kisses was ever the sweetest; the last smile the brightest; the last movement the gracefullest...no ill prospect has been able to turn your thoughts a moment from me...even if you did not love me I could not help an entire devotion to you: how much more deeply then must I feel for you knowing you love me..."

John Keats

Grow old along with me!
The best is yet to be,
The last of life, for which the first was made:

Our times are in his hand
Who saith, "A whole I planned,
Youth shows but half; trust God: see all, nor be
afraid!"...

Robert Browning, from "Rabbi Ben Ezra"

A thing of beauty is a joy forever:
Its loveliness increases; it will never
Pass into nothingness; but still will keep
A bower quiet for us, and a sleep
Full of sweet dreams...

John Keats

Sonnet XIV:

If thou must love me, let it be for nought
Except for love's sake only. Do not say,
'I love her for her smile—her look—her way
Of speaking gently,—for a trick of thought
That falls in well with mine, and certes brought
A sense of pleasant ease on such a day'—
For these things in themselves, Beloved, may
Be changed, or change for thee,—and love, so
wrought,
May be unwrought so. Neither love me for
Thine own dear pity's wiping my cheeks dry,—
A creature might forget to weep, who bore

Thy comfort long, and lose thy love thereby!
But love me for love's sake, that evermore
Thou mayest love on, through love's eternity.

Elizabeth Barrett Browning, from *Sonnets from the Portuguese*

...I give you my hand!
I give you my love more precious than money,
I give you myself before preaching or law;
Will you give me yourself? will you come travel with me?
Shall we stick by each other as long as we live?

Walt Whitman, from "Song of the Open Road"

If ever two were one, then surely we.
If ever man were lov'd by wife, then thee;
If ever wife was happy in a man,
Compare with me ye women if you can.
I prize thy love more than whole Mines of gold,
Or all the riches that the East doth hold.
My love is such that Rivers cannot quench,
Nor ought but love from thee, give recompence.
Thy love is such I can no way repay,
The heavens reward thee manifold I pray.
Then while we live, in love let's so persever,
That when we live no more, we may live ever.

Anne Bradstreet, from "To My Dear and Loving Husband"

Epilogue

You may help yourself to any of the vows or phrasings in this book; they are yours for the taking to mix and match at will. Or you may want to combine some of the phrasings found here with other prose or poetry you have gleaned from a love note or card received from your intended, or from your favorite love song or poem.

If you're searching for classical ideas and you didn't find exactly what you're looking for in Chapter 9, you may wish to consider the other writings of Elizabeth Barrett Browning, Robert Browning, William Shakespeare, Kahlil Gibran, James Russell Lowell, John Ciardi, E.E. Cummings, Gerard Manley Hopkins Carl Sandburg, James Joyce, John Keats, Percy Bysshe Shelley, Anne Bradstreet, Christopher Marlowe, Charles Dickens, Anne Morrow Lindbergh, Walt Whitman, Wendell Berry, Philip Sidney, William Penn,

Mark Twain, Henry Van Dyke, Robert Burns, John Donne, Martin Luther, Voltaire, Stephen Sondheim and, of course, the Bible.

As you compose your vows, however, whether they are contemporary or classical, consider these four questions:

- How do we feel about our unique relationship to each other?
- What are our hopes and dreams for our marriage?
- What words can we use to express these thoughts?
- Which format do we prefer? Monologue, dialogue or question and answer?

Your vows should reflect the deep emotional and spiritual bond between the two of you and the uniqueness of your own special relationship, which is like none other.

Have fun and God bless you as you create your own wedding vows!

Diane Warner

I will be updating this book in the years to come and I would appreciate a copy of your original wedding vows, if you would agree to share them with me. Please write me in care of my publisher:

Diane Warner
c/o Career Press, Inc.
P. O. Box 687
Franklin Lakes, NJ 07417

Bibliography

Batts, Sidney F. *The Protestant Wedding Sourcebook*. John Knox Press, 1993.

Cole, Harriette. *Jumping the Broom: The African-American Wedding Planner*. Henry Holt and Co., 1995.

Diamant, Anita. *The New Jewish Wedding*. Simon and Schuster, 1993.

Eklof, Barbara. *With These Words...I Thee Wed*. Bob Adams, 1989.

Glusker, David and Misner, Peter. *Words for Your Wedding*. HarperCollins, 1993.

Jones, Leslie. *Happy Is the Bride the Sun Shines On*. Contemporary Books, 1995.

Kehret, Peg. *Wedding Vows*. Meriwether Publishing Ltd., 1989.

Kingma, Daphne Rose. *Weddings from the Heart*. Conari Press, 1995.

Klausner, Abraham J. *Weddings: A Complete Guide to All Religious and Interfaith Marriage Services*. Alpha Publishing, 1986.

Latner, Helen. *Your Jewish Wedding*. Doubleday & Co., 1985.

Leviton, Richard. *Weddings by Design*. Harper, San Francisco, 1993.

Mbiti, John S. *African Religions and Philosophy*. Heineman, 1969.

Munro, Eleanor. *Wedding Readings*. Penguin Books USA, 1986.

Ronatree Green, Danita. *Broom Jumping: A Celebration of Love*. Entertaining Ideas, Ltd., 1992.